Classic Gatwick
PROPLINERS

CLASSIC GATWICK
PROPLINERS

TOM SINGFIELD

The
History
Press

First published 2019
Reprinted 2021

The History Press
97 St George's Place,
Cheltenham, Gloucestershire, GL50 3Qb
www.thehistorypress.co.uk

British Library Cataloguing in Publication Data.
A catalogue record for this book is available from the British Library.

ISBN 978 0 7509 8922 0

Typesetting and origination by The History Press
Printed and bound by TJ Books Limited, Padstow, Cornwall

CONTENTS

FOREWORD

As the son of a Battle of Britain pilot who went on to become a successful airline pilot, it was probably inevitable that I would grow up with a passion for aviation. This enabled me to travel in some of the wonderful aeroplanes depicted in this book, including a flight to Singapore as a monkey handler. My first memories of Gatwick were in the 1960s when Father worked for Ace Freighters flying Constellations and DC-4s. I used to visit their offices in a converted bungalow called Westpoint, from where I watched the aeroplanes pictured in this book and dreamt about the experiences the crews must have had and the dangers they sometimes faced. The author of this book, Tom Singfield, spent twenty-five years as an air traffic controller at Gatwick, and although our paths never crossed directly, there must have been occasions when I availed myself of his professional services.

I joined British Island Airways (BIA) at Gatwick as Financial Controller in 1970 and later learned to fly. BIA operated only propliners in those days, including the venerable Dakota and the Dart Herald. I remained with BIA until its demise in 1990 due to the vagaries of the economy and the duplicity of the banks, by which time I had become Chairman. I well remember the last flight of our DC-3s, flown by two pilots who were also retiring. Enough to say, they had a lot of fun! Tom Singfield's book has reminded me of those pilots who flew from Gatwick back in the pioneering days of the 1960s and 1970s; most were ex-military who had fought in the Second World War. Unfortunately many of them have now 'flown away', but the aircraft they flew from Gatwick are lovingly recorded here for posterity.

Peter Villa

INTRODUCTION

This book is a celebration of all the wonderful 'propliners' that operated from Gatwick for the first twenty years after its reopening in 1958. By the late 1970s, the majority of movements were flown by jetliners; the older propeller-powered types, such as the Viking, Hermes, Ambassador, Argonaut, Britannia, Bristol 170, Heron, Dove, Commando, Constellation, Convairliner, Canadair CL-44, Stratocruiser, DC-3, DC-4, DC-6 and DC-7, were mostly just memories with only the occasional sighting of a rare survivor. The author first visited Gatwick as a plane spotter in 1965, and once the delights of colour slide photography took hold, a quest to find quality slides of those early Gatwick visitors took my interest. This book is the result of that search.

airport. Granted a commercial licence in 1934, Gatwick Aerodrome remained as a grass airfield throughout the Second World War, when it played a vital role in the protection of the south-east of England as a base for a variety of fighter squadrons and as a maintenance base for the repair of Royal Air Force (RAF) aircraft.

After the war, with post-war commercial traffic on the increase, the owners invested £6.8 million to create the basic airport layout we still see today. The east–west concrete runway was laid in 1957, and with a brand-new terminal building connected to parking stands by a central covered finger, the new airport, the first in the world to have air, main road and trunk-line rail linkage, was opened officially by HM The Queen on 9 June 1958.

EARLY GATWICK

When Ronald Waters bought 90 acres of farmland adjacent to the Gatwick racecourse in 1930 in order to set up a private airfield, little did he know how that airfield would evolve over the next eighty-nine years to become the world's busiest single-runway

FIRST ARRIVALS

In the early hours of 17 May 1958, BEA Helicopters' Westland Whirlwind helicopter G-AOCF Sir Lionel, flown by Captain J. Reid, flew from Gatwick to the ridge of high ground at Russ Hill to place a red hazard beacon atop a 70ft tower built on the extended centreline of the runway. The job was filmed from another British European Airlines (BEA) helicopter. The beacon was 227ft above aerodrome level and 1¾ miles from the threshold of runway 09. The high ground at Russ Hill has had close calls with aircraft into and out of Gatwick over the years. One of the closest to a real disaster was on 2 September 1963 when an Iberia Super Constellation operating for AVIACO smashed through the treetops next to the beacon on a night approach to runway 09. Thankfully, it landed safely but the aircraft was damaged, with a landing light smashed, a propeller tip snapped off, hydraulic lines broken and various panels dented.

On 20 May 1958, an RAF Vickers Varsity with the radio callsign 'MOZZZ' carried out some 'runway testing' flights, which were probably instrument landing system (ILS) checks, and in preparation for the visit of the Queen for the opening ceremony, an immaculately turned-out de Havilland Heron of the RAF Queen's Flight (XM296) made a visit on 29 May so that the organising team could run through the opening ceremony and check out the airport and facilities. Flown by Wing Commander D.F. Hyland-Smith, Officer Commanding Queen's Flight, with Air Commodore Sir Edward 'Mouse' Fielden KCVO, Captain of the Queen's Flight aboard, it was met by around 100 pressmen who were being given a tour of the airport by Airport Commandant Brian Oakley.

Prior to the official opening, the new terminal at Gatwick had already seen some passengers as Transair Vickers Viscount G-AOXV had landed on a trooping flight from Malta on runway 27 with fifty-eight adults plus children on board at 3.45 on the afternoon of Friday, 30 May 1958. The same day, a Transair Viscount (probably G-AOXU) operated an inclusive tour flight to Nice on behalf of Horizon Holidays. Viscount G-AOYS of British European Airways was also parked on the apron that day. The first passenger to alight from G-AOXV was Mrs Pamela Morrison, wife of a Royal Navy submarine lieutenant from Broxbourne, Hertfordshire, carrying their 8-month-old son, Campbell. While the military families found their way home by train, bus or car, the Transair aircrew were whisked away in a Bentley! Another Transair Viscount with military families from Gibraltar went to London Heathrow, where the Morrisons had also expected to land. In 2017, the author set out to trace the new Gatwick's first official arriving passenger. Thanks to some guesswork involving the Royal Navy and an interest in boating, the author found Campbell living in Scotland, but sadly his mother had died. He had no idea he had played a small part in Gatwick's history and was delighted to discover this piece of his family history.

Within a year of opening, the airport had several British airlines operating 'inclusive tours' (IT) charters. Air Links had a DC-3 Dakota, African Air Safaris had two Vikings, Pegasus had Vikings and Derby Airways had Dakotas, all of them serving the ever-increasing demand for inclusive tours. Passenger numbers in the first seven months after the official opening were 186,172. The following full year saw 369,397, in 1965–66 it was 1,400,000 and by 1969 it had risen to an impressive 3,194,000.

Interestingly, the first foreign airline to operate from the new Gatwick was Sudan Airways. Arriving on 5 June 1959, its first 'Blue Nile' weekly schedule departed on 8 June in a sixty-one-seater Viscount 831, ST-AAN, that was bought new in early 1959 in a joint venture with British United Airways. The usual route for flight SD110 was Rome–Athens–Cairo–Khartoum.

Without waiting for the airport to be officially opened, on Saturday, 7 June, Transair commenced its summer DC-3 Dakota scheduled flights to Jersey. The next day saw Transair DC-3s G-AMZG and G-ANTB, plus CAFU Dove G-ALVS, parked on the apron.

OPENING DAY

Flown from Heathrow by Hyland-Smith with the Queen and Prince Philip aboard, the freshly polished Heron XM295 of the Queen's Flight landed at Gatwick at 10.40 a.m. on 9 June. It parked up on the north side of the pier (there was only one then), where

it could be seen by around 7,000 spectators who were corralled behind barriers on both sides of the taxiway and on the roof of the pier. Nearby on the north apron was a selection of airliners on display, which consisted of Viscounts G-AMOG *Robert Falcon Scott* of BEA and G-AOXV of Transair, Dove G-AJDP of Morton Air Services and Heron G-AORH *Duchess of Normandy* of Jersey Airways. Peter Masefield, the MD of Bristol Aircraft, had flown himself to the event in his modified DHC-1 Chipmunk G-AOTM, which was parked in front of the Transair Viscount. On the other side of the pier was a line-up of BEA DC-3 Dakotas waiting to depart to the Channel Islands and a BEA Sycamore helicopter G-AMWH *Sir Geraint*.

This press image shows the very first passengers to arrive at Gatwick walking to their buses after arriving from Malta on a military charter on 30 May 1958. First down the steps was Mrs W.I. Morrison, carrying her 8-month-old son, Campbell. Some detective work by the author in 2017 found Campbell alive and well in Scotland and totally unaware of his part in Gatwick history. (David Thaxter collection)

Here is an airport scene that is a rare occurrence these days. A group of happy spectators and spotters enjoy a day out on the north pier at Gatwick in 1964. Back in 1968, when Gatwick was in Surrey, 200,000 spectators visited during that year. Overt security and a lack of appreciation by the airport operators of the benefits that non-flying visitors can provide mean that very few spectators' viewing areas survive at UK airports in 2019. (John Kimberley)

The royal party was greeted on the apron by Lord Munster, the Lord Lieutenant of Surrey, and by the Minister of Transport and Civil Aviation, Harold Watkinson MP. Also present were Airey Neave MP, Parliamentary Secretary to the Minister, and the Airport Commandant. The party were invited to inspect a Guard of Honour consisting of ten airline captains. From BEA were P.J. McKeown, E.R.A. Roberts and P. Rowlands, from Transair were S.G. Webster, A.C. Lawson and R. Palmer, from Morton Air Services were Chief Pilot T.J. 'Ben' Gunn and Captain Frank Harper with B.W. Gardiner and J.A. Spencer from Jersey Airlines.

Once the hoo-ha had died down, BEA 'Pionair' DC-3 G-ALXK took off on a passenger charter to Jersey. Interestingly, BEA's first association with Gatwick was its helicopter division, which lived adjacent to the old 'Beehive' terminal in 1954–55. These initial BEA Dakota services were to the Channel Islands with up to seven flights to Guernsey and up to fourteen flights with either DC-3s or Viscounts to Jersey. Transair's first services from Gatwick were schedules to Jersey as well as newspaper flights, inclusive tours and trooping charters.

PROPLINERS AT GATWICK

The most common 'propliner' to grace the new Gatwick ramps from 1958 was the Douglas DC-3 Dakota. Services by BEA and Transair DC-3s, many of them to the Channel Islands, were there right from the opening day, while representing the jet-turbine airliner was the ground-breaking Vickers Viscount, which remained a Gatwick stalwart for the next twenty years. Remarkably, examples of both the DC-3 and Viscount were still making the occasional visit to London Gatwick into the 1990s.

Although the use of piston and turbine-powered 'propliners' was still thriving in the first years of the new Gatwick, the inevitable take-over by jet airliners was in evidence even in the early days. The first arrival of a pure jet airliner was on 16 November 1958 when the British Overseas Airways Corporation's (BOAC) de Havilland Comet G-APDC diverted into Gatwick from Heathrow. However, this was a rare occasion and the regular sight of a jet airliner on a scheduled service rather than a Heathrow diversion or a test flight did not come until December 1964 when BUA commenced a Gatwick to Santiago (Chile) schedule using its brand new VC10.

The first twenty years after the new Gatwick was opened in 1958 was a time of massive changes, with new airlines, new airliners, longer routes, more passenger facilities and ever-increasing passenger numbers. Up the road at Heathrow, where many flights were performed by government-owned airlines, the older airliner types were quickly being displaced by faster and more luxurious jetliners as each airline pressed forward with fleet renewals and longer routes. Back down at Gatwick, the pace was different and the type of services offered was less 'business meeting in New York' and more 'week in Majorca'. Gatwick was primarily a holiday airport and its airlines retained some classic piston and turbine 'propliners' as they were cheap and (mostly) reliable. Gatwick could always be relied on to provide some interesting and rare types from strange airlines and this was a big pull for the local enthusiasts, who never knew what they would find after climbing the stairs to the viewing decks and paying their entry fee.

SPECTATORS' VIEWING DECKS

One reason behind this book was the author's vivid memories of many hours spent watching the airport action (and inaction) from the excellent viewing decks situated on the roofs of the piers in the 1960s and '70s. These were superb vantage points for photography and many shots herein are from these spots. Rather than hanging around the fence by the General Aviation Terminal (GAT) or playing cricket or football on the grass, for a few pence dropped in a turnstile, you could spend a whole day wandering the viewing decks and get close up to the action. Refreshments were available from the infamous café run by Eddie, who was something of a celebrity amongst the spotting fraternity, or if you fancied a walk, you could hike up the A23 to the truckers' cafe at the Longbridge roundabout for pie, chips and beans. The original centre finger viewing deck remained open to spectators until around 1965; after that, only the north and south decks were accessible.

The British Airports Authority (BAA) took over the running of Gatwick in 1966 and continued to encourage non-flying visitors to watch the airport from the viewing decks. At one time, it announced that the spectators' viewing decks at Gatwick were the second busiest tourist attraction in the south-east of England after Brighton Pier! However, this golden era for spectators was not to last and the closure of the viewing decks on top of the north and south fingers in 1973 due to heightened security levels was a real blow to visitors. The BAA did build a nice new Skyview spectators' area in 1996 on an upper area of the South Terminal, but this was quite distant from the aircraft and not nearly as close to the action as the old decks had allowed. However, a lot of effort went into this project and there was a café, an enthusiasts' shop and even a complete HP Herald airliner and a de Havilland Comet nose to inspect. This popular facility for airport visitors was sadly shut down in September 2003 as the space was needed for further expansion of the South Terminal, and by then the airport owner was trying to discourage non-flying visitors from staying around the airport. The main terminal was a valuable piece of real estate and no place for enthusiasts or meeters and greeters to hang around. The Gatwick viewing experience for non-flyers was dead.

ACKNOWLEDGEMENTS
AND THANKS

This work would have been pretty slim if it was not for the skills and generosity of many photographers who have provided me with scans or loaned slides for me to process. I would like to thank the following who have either supplied images or helped with caption research: Adrian Balch, Ken Ede, Geoff Weir, Martin Fenner, Geoff Dobson, David Potter, Bob O'Brien, John Crawford, Peter Guiver, Terry Rattue, Bernard King, Steve Hill, Tony Hyatt, Keith Palmer, Dave Peace, Pierre-Alain Petit, Keith Dagwell, Tony Clarke, Brian Totman, Dave Freeman, Pete Waterfield, Tony Eastwood, Caz Caswell, Mike Axe, Bob Wall, Niall Booth, Keith Butcher, Ian Terry, Tim Spearman, Chris Knott and Peter Marson.

I would like to give my special thanks to Jacques Guillem in Paris, who has provided some wonderful Gatwick images from his incredible slide collection. Special thanks also to Tony Merton Jones and Pete Hillman for their knowledgeable help with the photo captions and to Harry Hawkins and John Dyer of the Gatwick Aviation Society for their help with captions and their impressive knowledge of early Gatwick aircraft movements. Thanks also to Peter Villa for kindly agreeing to write the foreword for this book.

Tom Singfield
Horsham,
October 2018

1
BUILT IN BRITAIN

British-built airliner types have always been a favourite of the author and it seems a shame that, with such an amazing aviation heritage, the UK no longer builds any commercial airliners. More than 6,000 airliners were built in the UK after the Second World War, with the last complete British-built airliner being an Avro RJ delivered in November 2003. Today, the UK's largest current commercial airliner project is the manufacture of Airbus wings. This chapter celebrates those days when Britain boasted a variety of 'propliner' manufacturers whose names for many are now just memories, namely Handley Page, Vickers, Avro, Bristol, de Havilland, Scottish Aviation and Airspeed. Their 'propliners', particularly the Vickers Viscount, could all once be seen at Gatwick, but sadly not any more.

A regular Gatwick visitor from 1965 to 1966 with Metropolitan Air Movements, Dove 5 G-AROI is seen here in the colours of Exeter-based British Westpoint Airlines at Gatwick on 24 May 1966. Metropolitan bought out British Westpoint in September 1965 but the airline, with DC-3s, Rapides, this Dove and a Heron, continued flying under its Westpoint name. G-AROI became *Eaglet* with British Eagle at Heathrow in June 1966 immediately after Westpoint's collapse. (Peter Keating via Tony Eastwood)

Seen dumped on the south-side grass area at Gatwick on 19 June 1965 after it had had been impounded by the Ministry of Civil Aviation for non-payment of landing fees, Trans-European's Bristol 170 'Wayfarer' was actually the prototype, first flown at Filton in December 1945. G-AGPV remained at Gatwick until September 1965, when it was scrapped. Trans-European Airlines (TEA) had started operations in 1959 at Swansea with a couple of DH Rapides, moving on to Coventry during the spring of 1960. TEA went on to fly two Lockheed 049E Constellations, but ran out of money with debts of £125,000 in 1962. (Author's collection)

Dan-Air London snapped up the fleet of three Airspeed Ambassadors from the Australian airline Butler Air Transport in November 1959. Repainted in Dan-Air colours and retaining the forty-nine seats originally fitted by BEA, they commenced flying services in March 1960. These initial IT services were flown from Blackbushe to Amsterdam, Brussels, Paris, Munich, Nice, Santander, Tarbes and Tours, while ad-hoc services including troop charters saw them land as far away as Gibraltar. Dan-Air moved to Gatwick in May 1960, with G-AMAH making the first charter to Munich and Zagreb on the 22nd. Dan-Air operated a total of eight Ambassadors without any major incidents; the last Ambassador flight was Jersey to Gatwick on 26 September 1971. (Brian Robbins)

This rare colour shot of the Sudan Airways Vickers Viscount 831 ST-AAN shows it parked in the maintenance area at Gatwick. Bought brand new in a joint venture with BUA in June 1959, it was officially registered to Airwork Ltd and leased immediately to Sudan Airways for its London–Khartoum service. The SD110/111 weekly schedule left Gatwick at midday on Monday and, routing via Rome, Athens and Cairo, arrived at Khartoum at 0450 the following morning. ST-AAN was often parked at Gatwick for a few days and during one such downtime it covered for the late arrival of Jersey Airlines' Heralds by making three rotations to Jersey on just one day, 17 June 1961. The London–Khartoum 'Blue Nile' service used this single Viscount until its final arrival at Gatwick on 8 December 1962. Repainted as G-ASED three days later, it officially went to Air Charter Ltd, but from June 1960 they had become part of British United Airways, so the aircraft flew in BUA colours. (Chris Knott collection)

The Silver City Airways Handley Page Hermes fleet moved from Manston to Gatwick during the spring of 1962. Hermes 4A G-ALDU made its last Gatwick movement on 10 October 1962 when it left for the short flight to Stansted, where it was scrapped. Why Silver City? Back in 1946, the Zinc Corporation (owners of the airline) was headquartered at Broken Hill in New South Wales, a town popularly known as 'Silver City' because of its silver mines. The five Silver City Hermes were originally used for the London–Paris 'Silver Arrow' service, which was launched in June 1959 and actually flew Manston to Le Touquet, with the rest of the service using trains. Other Silver City types to use Gatwick were the Dove, Heron, Douglas DC-3 and Bristol Freighter. (Author's collection)

A nice line-up of two de Havilland Herons and a Handley Page Herald carrying British United Island Airways logos parked by Stand 1 in October 1969. Gatwick regular G-ANWZ, nearest to the camera, had previously carried Jersey Airlines titles and first appeared with them way back in November 1958. It later flew for Morton Air Services before joining the BUA brand in 1968. Note the fixed undercarriage of both of these early Series 1B Herons and the BUA Viscount and VC10 over in the maintenance area. The route over there from the main ramp was via the Maintenance Taxiway visible in the background. Despite this taxiway being clear of the runway threshold, controllers had to stop aircraft movements on it if traffic was landing on 27 or departing on 09. (Mike Axe collection)

Looking rather tired and frozen, tied down on the grass at Gatwick on 6 March 1965, is Scottish Aviation Twin Pioneer 9L-LAC of Sierra Leone Airways (SLA). BUA registered two second-hand Twin Pioneers after it took a 70 per cent stake in SLA in 1961, and both G-APRS and G-APMT passed through Gatwick on delivery early that year. G-APMT, which was reportedly an independence gift from the British government, returned to Gatwick in August 1962 as 9L-LAC *Freetown*, and also came back a couple of times in 1964 and 1965, probably for maintenance. It was donated to the Nepalese Royal Flight in July 1965. (Robin Ridley)

Irish-registered Aer Turas (Gaelic for Air Tours) Bristol 170 Freighter EI-APC made several visits to Gatwick in the summer of 1966, followed by a single visit in 1967 when it was photographed outside the Air Couriers hangar on 10 July. Bought from BKS Air Transport in March 1966, EI-APC was one of two 'Biffos' in the fleet and stayed active with them for six years before being sold in France. Used for transporting livestock, the Freighter was greeted by some very unkind comments about its looks from other aircrew on the R/T, particularly the Americans who had never seen such a strange bird. Sistership EI-APM never came to Gatwick and was written off in a fatal crash at Dublin on 12 June 1967. The company operated a variety of types, including DC-3, DC-4, DC-7, DC-8, CL-44, Argosy, Britannia and TriStar, and eventually closed down in July 2003. (Author's collection)

It was always nice to see a de Havilland Heron carrying full non-airline company titles. This Series 2D Heron G-ARTI was bought new in September 1961 by E.S. & A. Robinson (Holdings) Limited, which was a Bristol-based printing and packaging company founded in 1844. The Heron, given the name *ESANDAR*, a play on the company name, was used to ferry company executives and technicians around Europe from its base at Filton, and made many visits to Gatwick between 1963 and 1967. Sold in France in January 1970 as F-BRSK, it became part of the Air Paris fleet and continued to visit Gatwick. Robinsons merged with John Dickinson Stationery to form the Dickinson Robinson Group (DRG) in 1966 and bought Morton's old Heron 2D G-AOGO in 1969. (Jacques Guillem collection)

Royal Canadian Air Force Bristol Freighter Mk.31M 9700 was a very regular visitor to Gatwick, making over 120 visits. First arriving in July 1962, it is seen here on 9 September 1965 in much need of a fresh coat of paint, about to taxi out for its return to the Canadian base at Marville in France. It was assigned to 137th Transport Flight based at Baden-Soellingen RCAF Station, supporting Canadian Army troops based in the Sauerland/West Germany. It last visited Gatwick in December 1966 en route to Weston-super-Mare to be civilianised for Wardair Canada as CF-WAG. In 1970, it sank through the ice of a lake in Canada and was never recovered. (Adrian Balch collection)

This retired Handley Page Hermes fuselage became a true landmark at Gatwick, as for many years it was a sight that thousands of motorists saw while driving along the A23 past the airport. G-ALDG was retired from service by Silver City Airways and arrived at Gatwick in 1962, where it was dismantled and mounted on a cradle outside the offices of British United Airways for use as a cabin trainer. This shot was taken in May 1966. Later it was repainted in the sandstone and blue BUA colours and after that in British Caledonian colours. Once its use as a cabin trainer finished, it was hauled over to the fire service training ground behind the control tower for smoke evacuation training. In 1981, this last surviving remnant of the Hermes went into preservation at the Duxford museum. (Peter Keating)

Originally part of the massive BOAC Britannia fleet from 1958, Bristol Britannia 312 G-AOVS was converted to a 312F freighter in June 1966 by Lloyd International. Bought by Redcoat Air Cargo primarily for services to West Africa and named *Christian* after owner Mike Owen's son, it entered service with a trip from its base at Luton to Accra in May 1977. A second Redcoat Britannia, G-BRAC, was destroyed in a crash at Boston, USA, in February 1980. The fuselage of G-AOVS still resides at Luton, where it was used by the fire service for training. (Author's collection)

This Series 2A Hawker Siddeley 748 first flew as G-AVRR in September 1967 and went on to have a very interesting career under the ownership of the manufacturer in its role as a company demonstrator. First leased to SATA Air Açores in 1969, it later flew for Skyways-Coach Air, Transair Canada, Olympic Airways, Air Afrique, Air Cape, Zambia Airways, South African Airways, Merpati Airlines and Trans Gabon before it was sold to Eastern Provincial Airways (EPA) in Newfoundland, Canada, in March 1976 as a replacement for its HP Heralds on the route to Iles-de-la-Madeleine. Seen here on its delivery flight, which routed Tel Aviv, Athens, Marseilles, Gatwick, Prestwick, Keflavik and Gander that month, it flew with EPA until December 1981, when it crashed into the terminal building at Sydney, Nova Scotia, after the nosewheel steering failed. It had clocked up a total time of 15,186 hours and a very impressive 21,730 landings. (John Crawford)

The surviving control tower logbooks kept at The History Centre in Woking, Surrey, show that many of the Overseas Aviation fleet of nine Vickers Vikings were regulars at Gatwick during the period between June 1960 and its collapse in August 1961. The airline had moved its fleet of Vikings and Argonauts from Southend into a new Scandinavian-designed wooden hangar at Gatwick costing £300,000. The huge hangar was the largest clear-span timber building in the UK. Overseas became very busy on IT flights, but serious financial problems arose in 1961 and on 13 August British Petroleum (BP) shut off all fuel supplies to Overseas due to non-payment of bills. With the company on the brink of collapse, the following day, Overseas Viking G-AJCE was written off in a crash in France and within hours the airline shut up shop, leaving the illustrated G-AHPJ as one of four complete and two dismantled Vikings in the Gatwick base. (Author's collection)

Saunders flew its second prototype ST-27 commuter liner CF-XOK to Gatwick on 14 May 1970 after it had appeared at the Hanover Air Show. The aircraft was demonstrated to a number of British airlines, including Dan-Air, which was seeking a replacement for its DC-3 fleet. Built at Gimli, Manitoba, the type was an extensively modified de Havilland Heron, with the most obvious difference being the use of two 715 eshp UACL PT-6A-27 turbine engines rather than the Heron's usual four Gipsy Queen piston engines. Sadly, only thirteen examples of this promising conversion were completed. The price for a new ST-27 delivered to the UK was quoted as £177,000. (Author's collection)

After the unfortunate accident that wrote off Decca's immaculate Vickers Valetta at Gatwick in September 1963, the generous insurance company payout allowed Decca to purchase this Airspeed Ambassador G-ALZP from Morocco, where it had been King Hassan's personal transport. The Ambassador had been recommended for Decca's use by George Errington, who had been a senior test pilot for Airspeed. He negotiated the deal for a reported £28,000 and after six weeks' work at Air Couriers it went into service. Decca certainly got a bargain, as it continued to fly the Ambassador until it departed Gatwick for storage at West Malling in July 1970. Sold to a 'paper' airline in New Zealand in 1971, much time and money went into its restoration, but apart from a single test flight it never flew again and was scrapped in 1973. (Author's collection)

In early 1958, the small West African country of Sierra Leone commenced internal services with three DH Dragon Rapides operated by Sierra Leone Airways. After the agreement by BUA to run the airline in 1961, the Rapides were replaced with a pair of Twin Pioneers and then Herons on domestic scheduled services. This Heron 1B, 9L-LAG, was initially leased, then purchased, from Morton Air Services and is seen here in April 1970 stuffed full of seats back at Gatwick for some maintenance. SLA operated a total of four Herons, all of them returning to Gatwick for servicing through to the 1970s. (Author's collection)

After Swiss airline Globe Air went out of business in 1967, a couple of former staff helped to form African Safari Airways in order to continue their passenger flights to Nairobi (Kenya) and Entebbe (Uganda) from Zurich. The illustrated Britannia was a Series 307 when it first appeared at Gatwick on 1 December 1959 in the colours of British airline Air Charter Ltd as G-ANCD. The following year it was a regular at Gatwick with British United, and at the time this shot was taken of its landing at Gatwick in January 1976, it was owned by Gemini Air Cargo and leased to African Safari still in its previous International Aviation Services colours as a fully cargo-configured Series 307F. Mombasa-based African Safari owned seven different Britannias, including 5X-UVH and 5X-UVT, registered in Uganda. The cockpit section of 5Y-AYR still exists in Burnham-on-Sea. (Author's collection)

A very rare visitor on 13 May 1961 was this anonymous-looking Series 839 Vickers Viscount EP-MRS on its delivery flight from Wisley. Sold to the government of Iran for VIP use by the Shah, it departed Gatwick en route to Frankfurt on the 15th. Note that it is fitted with 'slipper' fuel tanks on the wings; it also had a main door retractable airstair. In 1963 the Iran government leased it to the national airline Iran Air, which later sold it to the Royal Australian Air Force (RAAF). It passed through Gatwick again on 16 September 1970 as VH-EQQ after the RAAF sold it to the USA. It then flew for a succession of operators including the Sultan of Oman's Air Force, Royal Swazi National Airways, Air Bridge Carriers and finally Dan-Air London, which based it at Teesside as G-BGLC flown by ABC crews. The aircraft still existed in Zimbabwe in 2016 after use as a restaurant. (Author's collection)

One of only two Senegalese-registered aircraft to be seen at Gatwick was this DH Dove 6V-ABT; the other was the government-operated Boeing 727 6V-AEF in 1988. The Dove was previously British-registered G-ANAN with Morton Air Services, and was painted up in Air Senegal colours at Gatwick on 23 May 1969. A couple of weeks later it departed for Toussus on its delivery flight. It lasted a couple of years in Africa before being scrapped. Compagnie Sénégalalse de Transportes Aériens (Air Senegal) was formed in November 1962 at Dakar-Yoff Airport for domestic and international services, aircraft maintenance, air taxi and charter work. The initial fleet included a Twin Pioneer leased from Sierra Leone Airways and by 1968 the airline had three DC-3s, one Dove, three Aztecs, one Navajo and two Cherokee Sixes. Over the years, Air Senegal operated eleven different DH Doves. (Author's collection)

Gatwick spectators who were happy to pay sixpence for entry to the viewing decks back in the 1960s could get super views such as this, while many enthusiasts and members of the general public were happy to park their car/motorbike/cycle by the fence in the background and sit on the grass to watch the aircraft. Many a game of football or cricket passed the time between aircraft movements, but it was difficult to get your ball back if it went on to the apron! Falconair's Viscount 784D SE-CNK was delivered in May 1967 to join SE-CNL and SE-CNM, which had arrived in April. SE-CNK was photographed on its first visit to Gatwick on 22 July on a return service from Malmö. In February 1968, Falconair launched a regular Saturday service to Gatwick from Stockholm, and that summer additional Viscount flights were made to Gothenburg. (Bernard King)

Swiss airline Globe Air was formed in Bern on 9 March 1957 in order to increase local tourism. It bought a forty-nine-seater Airspeed Ambassador from BEA in November 1960 and in the following January commenced IT charters from Switzerland to Spain and Madeira and from the UK to Switzerland. Two more Ambassadors were acquired with all three, HB-IEK, HB-IEL and HB-IEM, making appearances at Gatwick before modernisation with turboprops arrived in the shape of two Handley Page Heralds in 1963. The first visit of a Globe Air

Herald was on 1 May 1963 when HB-AAG was delivered from Radlett to Basle via Gatwick. The illustrated HB-AAK was delivered via the same route on 13 March 1964. The four-strong Herald fleet was kept busy on routes to Gatwick, especially ski charters in the winter. Globe Air later bought two Bristol Britannias for long-haul charters (they also visited Gatwick), but they never recovered after one crashed at Nicosia in April 1967 with the loss of 126 lives, and the airline collapsed in October that year. (Author's collection)

RAF Royal Flight HS 748 Andovers made several visits to Gatwick, but the aircraft's big brother, the HS680 Andover, was a very rare arrival. About to taxi out is Andover C.1 XS609 of the RAF Air Support Command on 24 May 1970. It carries the crest of RAF 46 Squadron on the fin and the Coat of Arms of Abingdon on the nose. This particular Andover came to a sticky end on 8 April 1972 while carrying the RAF Falcons parachute team on take-off at Siena, Italy, killing four passengers after cartwheeling and catching fire on take-off. (Author's collection)

Founded at Coventry Airport in 1970, cargo charter airline Midland Air Cargo (MAC) had some big names behind it, with Lord Trefgarne and the Marquis of Headfort putting up the money. Bristol Superfreighters G-APAV and G-AMLP were the first to join the fleet, with the illustrated G-APAU *City of Edinburgh* being bought from British Air Ferries in March 1971. Although it announced that it would buy four HS Argosies from Canada in late 1972, the deal collapsed with MAC in financial difficulties and the company folded in early 1973. (Tony Eastwood collection)

This very early 1947-built de Havilland Dove 2B with a rare Pakistan registration, AP-AGJ, was originally G-AKJR with Olley Air Service. Sold to Pakistan Petroleum Limited in April 1953, it returned to Gatwick from Karachi in February 1960 and made a few flights over the next three years before disappearing in 1963. Reappearing at Gatwick on April Fool's Day 1965, it sat outside Morton's hangar and never flew again. It was dismantled and on 21 September 1967 it was taken by road to Southend where Channel Airways was planning to convert a number of Doves to Carstedt CJ-600 configuration. This proposal never came to fruition and the aircraft was scrapped. (Author's collection)

An airline forever associated with Gatwick is Laker Airways. Founded by Freddie Laker, the former managing director of British United Airways, it acquired two former BOAC Britannias, G-ANBM and G-ANBN, that had been in storage at Cambridge for years. *Bravo Mike*, seen here in 1969, flew Laker's first commercial service on 29 July 1966. Laker had bravely ordered brand new BAC 1-11 'jetliners', and the first of these commenced IT charters from Gatwick and Manchester to Mediterranean resorts in March 1967. Laker was a major player at Gatwick for many years, but sadly his airline went bankrupt in 1982. Note the distant 'propliners', comprising DC-7, Constellation, Viscount, Britannia and Ambassador. (Martin Fenner collection)

No, not the Decca Record Company, but its sister company, the Decca Navigator Company, operated this ex-RAF Vickers Valetta G-APKR for trials, research, calibration and demonstrations of its aircraft navigation equipment from 1958 to 1963. Initially, Decca borrowed an RAF Valetta from the Ministry of Supply (MoS), as its Avro Anson was not large enough to carry all the gear and technicians for a new Doppler navigation device for the RAF. When the loan expired, Decca bought two Valettas from the MoS; one became G-APKR and the other (allocated G-APKS) was used as a source of spare parts at Biggin Hill. G-APKR made the first of very many appearances at Gatwick in January 1959. After landing at Gatwick in late September 1963, the starboard undercarriage collapsed and the aircraft was declared a write-off. The insurance money allowed Decca to buy an Airspeed Ambassador. (Chris Knott collection)

Jersey Airlines upgraded its fleet of de Havilland Dragon Rapide biplanes with brand new Herons from 1953 onwards. G-ANWZ *Duchess of Sark* was a Series 1B with fixed undercarriage, bought new in 1955 for scheduled services from Gatwick to Jersey. Jersey Airlines were one of the first operators to use the new Gatwick, and services commenced from the summer of 1958 using Herons and the occasional Bristol Freighter. The Herons, and later Dakotas, were very common sights until May 1961 when the airline's HP Heralds started to appear at Gatwick, leaving the Herons on other routes such as Manchester–Jersey, Southampton–Alderney, and services connecting the Channel Islands with north-western France. (Brian Stainer)

Previously known as African Air Safaris, Air Safaris had been around in various guises since 1950. In late 1959, with extensive IT services from Gatwick planned in the 1960 holiday season, the airline transferred its main operations base from Southend to Gatwick, whilst establishing a maintenance base at Hurn. Its fleet then consisted of a couple of Vickers Vikings and a single Handley Page Hermes. 1960 saw expansion with additional Vikings and another Hermes, while in 1961 further Hermes were bought from Skyways together with several additional Vikings. Series 627 Viking G-AJFT was delivered in April 1960 in this rather smart green and orange scheme, but it did not last long as the company folded with debts of over £500,000 in November 1961. (Peter Keating via Tony Eastwood collection)

Friday, 23 June 1961 saw the one and only visit to Gatwick of the Itavia DH Heron I-AOGO *Citta di Roma*. She departed back to Italy five days later. Aerolinee Itavia was founded by private investors in April 1958 and started scheduled domestic services with DH Doves and Herons the following year. The airline went on to operate the DC-3 and Dart Herald, both types being Gatwick regulars, and by the early 1970s, it had moved over to pure jets with F28s and DC-9-10s, which continued to visit Gatwick until the airline ceased flying in 1980. I-AOGO later flew with operators in the UK, Germany and Israel before ending up in Puerto Rico. (Brian Stainer)

In 1959, the local authorities at the newly opened airport at Bristol Lulsgate approached Dan-Air and asked if it would set up some scheduled domestic and European services. Dan-Air therefore bought two DH Dove 1Bs (G-ALVF and G-AIWF), with G-AIWF flying the first service, Lulsgate to Liverpool, on 4 April 1960. The illustrated G-ALVF was bought from the College of Aeronautics at Cranfield in January 1960 and flown to Dan-Air's maintenance base at Lasham in Hampshire by Captain Arthur Larkman. The eight-seater was painted in full Dan-Air London colours and commenced schedules from Lulsgate alongside G-AIWF. It made its first visit to Gatwick in Dan-Air service on 10 February 1960, flying Lasham–Gatwick–Blackbushe on a crew training sortie. (Mike Axe collection)

One of only two Viscounts operated by Manston-based Invicta Airways Ltd, Viscount 755D G-AOCC was purchased from British Eagle in February 1968. It was named *Sylt* because of its use on IT charters to this holiday island in Germany from its base at Berlin in the summer of 1968. Invicta had been occasional visitors to Gatwick from 1965 with DC-4s and the odd Vickers Viking, but for the 1968 summer season the Viscounts plied regularly to Basle, Gerona, Mahon, Munich and Palma. G-AOCC was transferred to British Midland Airways in 1969, when it was found to have serious wing corrosion and was scrapped at Castle Donington in 1970. (Jacques Guillem collection)

Bristol Britannia Series 317 G-APNB was bought by Gatwick-based Donaldson from BUA in October 1967 and named *Carillon* after the airline owner Tom Geekie's wife. It was immediately leased to Lloyd International and did not enter Donaldson service until April 1969. The other three Donaldson Britannias were also named, G-AOVF *Nike* after Geekie's daughter, and G-AOVC *Mikado* and G-APNA *Juno* after Nike's showjumping horses. All four flew IT charters from Gatwick and Glasgow as well as transatlantic charters from Gatwick and Prestwick. (Author's collection)

With its distinctive oval passenger door open for business, this British United V.708 Vickers Viscount G-ARBY was photographed at Gatwick in the early 1960s. This was the tenth of 444 Viscounts built, and it originally flew for Air France from 1953. In 1960–61 it was one of three Viscounts based at Gatwick with Maitland Drewery Aviation Ltd, flying IT services to destinations including Rome, Dublin and Munich. BUA acquired it in 1962 and the following year it suffered a landing accident at Gatwick early in the morning of 8 February, causing the runway to be closed for much of the day. In July 1980 it was written off after running out of fuel near Exeter Airport while flying for Alidair. (Chris Knott collection)

Owned by Air Bridge Carriers, Viscount 808 G-BBDK was leased to Dan-Air London in March 1975 in full passenger configuration and mostly used for the Lydd–Beauvais service. Once the season finished, *Delta Kilo* returned to ABC and by December it was back flying freight. Dan-Air leased other Viscounts including G-ARBY, G-ARGR and G-ARIR from Alidair, and G-BCZR and G-BGLC from Fields/ABC. (Bernard King)

One of five African Safari Airways Bristol Britannias, Series 314 5Y-ANS started life as a passenger airliner with Canadian Pacific Air Lines in 1958. Subsequently operated from Gatwick as G-ATMA with Caledonian Airways from 1965 onwards, on 4 April 1971 it flew from Gatwick to Luton for overhaul. It returned on the 27th as 5Y-ANS in African Safari Airways (ASA) colours, although it was actually owned by International Aviation Services. The two original Britannias with ASA were registered in Uganda as 5X-UVH and UVT. African International took over the lease in February 1972 and used it for freight-only services to Africa, even though it never received the large forward freight door. It is seen here in May that year about to be restored as G-ATMA. After retirement it was used as a source of spare parts at Biggin Hill before succumbing to the scrap man in 1975. (Bernard King collection)

Long-serving French carrier Compagnie Air Transport (CAT) leased this Mk.32 Bristol Superfreighter from original operator Silver City Airways, initially using its British registration G-ANWH before becoming F-BLHH *Dix-Huit Juin*. This '18 June' name marks the appeal made by Charles de Gaulle to the French people to continue their fight against the occupying forces in the Second World War. Other CIE Bristols also carried significant dates: F-BKBD and F-BKBG were both *Quatorze Juillet* after the storming of the Bastille and French National Day, and F-BKBI was *Onze Novembre* after Armistice Day 1918. F-BLHH was written off at Le Touquet in July 1969 when it was rammed by an airport excavator; however, it got a reprieve from the breakers, going on static display at Dieppe for several years. CAT aircraft were more usually seen at Lydd on cross-Channel services, so this was a rare visit to Gatwick. CAT also operated ATL-98 Carvairs, which also made a few visits to Gatwick. (John Mounce)

This classic Gatwick shot taken from the south finger shows Cambrian/BAS Viscount 701 G-AMON in 1970. This Viscount made its first visit to Gatwick on a Heathrow diversion on 25 November 1958 in BEA colours. Delivered to the Cambrian base at Cardiff-Rhoose in 1963, it did a stint with BOAC in Scotland in the early 1970s named *Scottish Princess*, becoming one of only two Viscounts to carry full BOAC colours (the other was G-AMOG). Parts of this long-serving aircraft still existed among the British Air Ferries Viscounts at Southend in 1982. (Bernard King)

You can almost hear the sound of the Rolls-Royce Dart turboprops in this lovely action shot of Dan-Air's Hawker Siddeley 748 G-AXVG in August 1972. It displays the Link City titles that referred to Dan-Air's internal schedules, which can be traced back to 1960 when it flew DH Doves from Bristol to Liverpool and Newcastle via Cardiff. Visible in the background is the BCAL Vickers VC10 G-ARTA, which was badly damaged in a hard landing the previous year. It never flew again. (Author's collection)

This lovely evocative photo taken from the south finger on 19 June 1973 well illustrates the Gatwick of the early 1970s, complete with a London Country Routemaster bus travelling north along the A23. The BEA experiment with regional divisions for domestic services from April 1971 saw large 'Scottish Airways' or 'Channel Islands' titles appear next to the BEA fuselage logo on some Viscount 802s. Initially BEA sent eight Viscounts to be based at Glasgow under the Scottish Airways banner, while the remaining twelve became Channel Islands, with four of these being based in Jersey, five in Birmingham, one in Guernsey, and two chartered to GB Airways for Gibraltar schedules. When BEA became part of British Airways in that momentous year for British commercial aviation of 1974, the large regional names stayed, but with the addition of a small 'British Airways' title on the lower fuselage, as in this image. Late in 1973, the Scottish Airways titles on G-AOHS were switched to British Airways, but *Hotel Sierra* never made it into later British Airways livery, as it was taken out of service at Cardiff in 1975 and ended up being burnt by the airport fire service for training. The last British Airways Viscount flight to the Channel Islands from London Gatwick was on 31 March 1980. (Brian Nicholls)

Austrian Airlines operated a total of twelve Viscounts, six Series 700 and six Series 800s, including V.837 OE-IAM *L.v.Beethoven* seen here on 17 July 1967 while on lease to Austrian Air Transport (AAT) from Austrian Airlines in full Austrian colours. Austrian Airlines owned 40 per cent of AAT, which was the charter subsidiary of the national airline. AAT also operated Viscounts OE-LAG and OE-LAK on lease from the parent airline. OE-IAM first flew as OE-LAM in July 1960, the reason for its altered registration being its lease to AAT in 1964. AAT flew charters and inclusive tour flights to destinations in Europe, Africa, the Middle East and various Mediterranean resorts. It flew four times weekly to Gatwick in the summer seasons of the 1960s, using 'OB' flight numbers. It used Viscounts up to and including 1968, switching to Caravelles for the summer of 1969. This aircraft survived until 1972, when it crashed in Colombia. (Author's collection)

The first aircraft to be owned by the newly formed African Safari Airways in late 1967 was this Ugandan-registered Britannia 313 5X-UVH. Painted in this distinctive livery with zebra-striped fin at Luton, it flew down to Gatwick on 30 December 1967 for 2½ hours of crew training 'circuits and bumps' before departing for ASA's European base at Zurich. The next day this former Globe Air Britannia flew its first service with a load of tourists bound for Nairobi and Mombasa – destinations visited regularly during its Globe Air service. On 19 July 1968, 5X-UVH commenced full passenger services from Gatwick to Nairobi, Mombasa and Entebbe via a fuel stop at Benina. It was re-registered in Kenya as 5Y-ALT at Gatwick on 24 May 1970, and in 1973 it was transferred to African Cargo Airways. (Author's collection)

This Bristol Superfreighter G-AMLP first appeared at Gatwick in 1959 with Air Charter, the following year it flew Gatwick services for Channel Air Bridge and by 1963 it was appearing at Gatwick carrying British United Air Ferries (BUAF) colours. Seen here in July 1968, G-AMLP *Vanguard* was built originally as a standard Mk.31 Freighter with a short nose and square-topped fin. In 1958 it was converted to Mk.32 Superfreighter with a 5ft nose extension and modified fin to enable it to carry three cars and twenty passengers or two larger vehicles and twelve passengers, the passenger seats being in the rear section of the fuselage. G-AMLP's visits to Gatwick were more often on bloodstock charters. It ended its days with Lambair in Canada when it crashed there in 1977. (Pierre-Alain Petit collection)

Imagine the glorious sound of eight Rolls-Royce Dart engines whistling away while this pair of Viscount 833s (G-APTC and G-APTD) wait at the easterly holding point, one evening in July 1969. Both were originally flown by Hunting Clan Air Transport from 1959 and were regulars at Gatwick. Once they were absorbed into the mighty BUA empire in 1960, they continued to fly from Gatwick for nearly ten years. Many enthusiasts, including myself, consider this sandstone and blue colour scheme to be one of the nicest to grace the ramp at Gatwick. (Pete Waterfield)

Having dropped off its passengers at Stand 1, Morton Air Services' de Havilland Dove G-AMYO is about to taxi over to the hangars. Founded by Captain T.W. Morton in May 1945, the airline bought two Dragon Rapides the following year and commenced charters from Croydon Airport. When Croydon closed in 1959, Mortons had a fleet of Rapides, Doves and Herons, and the whole outfit moved to Gatwick, where they flew successfully until they were fully absorbed into the BUA empire in November 1968. For many years Morton also flew its own network of scheduled services, linking Gatwick with Alderney, Brawdy and Swansea, together with other services to Exeter and the Channel Islands. (Author's collection)

The executive transport fleet of the Dutch electronics company Philips first arrived at Gatwick from their base at Eindhoven way back in December 1958 when Dove PH-ILI dropped in. Other early types operated included a Beech 18 and this Heron 2E PH-ILA, which appeared in January 1960. Another Heron, PH-ILO, was bought in 1960, and over the years most of the expanding Philips Vliegdienst fleet made visits to Gatwick with types such as Kingair, Baron and various Dassault business jets. Largest in the fleet was F.27 Friendship PH-LIP, which operated the company 'milk run' between Eindhoven and Gatwick. This service became so busy that Philips encouraged Dutch domestic airline NLM to take over the route from April 1974. (Ian Terry)

Dan-Air bought Ashford-based Skyways International in the spring of 1972 for £650,000 and acquired its four Series 100 HS748s. These were given Dan-Air Skyways titles while retaining the Skyways cheatline, and were immediately put into scheduled service including the cross-Channel coach-air services from Ashford to Beauvais. The illustrated G-AZSU never flew with Skyways, but when acquired in April 1972 it was given the Skyways cheatline to match the fleet. This hybrid colour scheme only lasted until the summer of 1973, when the aircraft were given the standard Dan-Air London red cheatline/red tail colours. (Author's collection)

It is the background of this shot of Autair's Airspeed Ambassador G-ALZZ that makes the author smile. This nostalgic scene was taken on Sunday afternoon, 9 July 1967. The Ambassador has just pulled up on to Stand 38 and is about to be visited by the customs man in his crisp white shirt, while the less-than-clean engineer prepares to plug in a ground power unit. G-ALZZ had flown in on a rare visit to Gatwick from its base at Luton to fly a charter to Ibiza, which departed at 0452. It was back at Gatwick at 1503 and airborne empty for Luton within the hour. In the background outside the fence, families watch the action, having parked their cars for free on the roadside, aircraft spotters sit on the grass next to their bicycles waiting for the next movement and the official terminal car park is packed with classic British-built cars. In the background can be seen a Swiss-registered Falco HB-UOB, Beagle 206 G-ATKP, Piper Twin Comanche G-ASJM and Beech Twin Bonanza N4379D. (Bob Wall)

Airnautic's Viking F-BJER made more than fifty visits to Gatwick on behalf of Air France from 1960 to 1963. The Perpignan-based company was a Gatwick regular from 1959 with its fleet of Vickers Vikings, and from the summer of 1962 Airnautic DC-6s started to appear. The following summer season saw the airline flying to Gatwick several times a week with up to five flights on a Saturday, mainly serving Nice, Perpignan and Toulouse. As well as Vikings and DC-6s, Airnautic's DC-4s also operated to Gatwick, and on rare occasions its magnificent Boeing 307 Stratoliners, F-BELY and F-BELU, made an appearance, probably the only time an aircraft of this type graced the ramp at London Gatwick. By 1964, the Vikings had gone and only the DC-6s and DC-4s appeared. The illustrated Viking F-BJER departed Gatwick for Perpignan on 11 September 1963 but crashed in the Pyrenees, killing all forty aboard. A week later, Airnautic DC-4 F-BBDH repatriated the bodies of the British passengers to Gatwick. (Author's collection)

One of aviation's little mysteries. On the morning of 17 October 1968, this Viscount Series 814 D-ANOL arrived at Gatwick from Frankfurt. Over the following three hours it made seven touch-and-goes before parking up on the North Park, where it stayed until returning to Frankfurt the following evening. It would not have flown all that way just to carry out training flights, so the author's guess is that it was being demonstrated to a potential buyer (perhaps Invicta?) in the UK. It had been leased to Condor Flugdienst by owner Lufthansa, which parked it up that November, and in January 1969 it was sold to British Midland Airways as G-AWXI. No other Condor Viscount visited Gatwick. (Richard Hunt collection)

Based at Shoreham Airport, the world's oldest licensed airfield, South Coast Air Services started in 1963 with a Dragon Rapide. It leased Heron 1B G-ANCI in 1965 from Lord Calthorpe and it first appeared at Gatwick on 8 March on a Shoreham–Gatwick–Shoreham flight. Its first commercial service was two days later when it flew a charter Gatwick–Jersey–Gatwick. It bought two Dakotas and both G-AJHZ and G-AMSN flew to Gatwick that year before the company folded on 5 August. In 1966, the airline's chairman commenced DC-3 charter flights from Gatwick with a new company, Irelfly. (Peter Keating via Tony Eastwood collection)

Bristol Britannia 314 G-ATMA was delivered from Southend to Gatwick for Caledonian Airways on 6 January 1966 and departed on its first service the following day to Khartoum. Photographed in October 1970, like others in the seven-strong Caledonian Britannia fleet, it carries the name of a Scottish County, in this case *County of Midlothian*, in the yellow cheat line. These 'Brits' were mainly used on transatlantic charters and later European IT services. Note the spectators on the North Pier behind and the small glass-sided hut to hide in when the weather was bad. The author spent many happy hours on these piers in the late 1960s, but it could be quite tedious with sometimes over an hour between movements. (Mike Axe collection)

Who doesn't love the classic colour scheme on this DH Heron F-BRSK at Gatwick in September 1971? Previously G-ARTI, it was named *Ville du Havre* in Air Paris service and used for scheduled services from Paris Orly to Le Havre, Le Mans and Gatwick. By 1973, the airline had switched to a Beech 99 and Twin Otter and had added Paris to Rouen, Paris to Les Sables d'Olonne, Rouen to Gatwick, Le Havre to Gatwick, Paris to Royan and Paris to Angoulême. Note the tail logo 'AP' used the Eiffel Tower as the letter 'A'. (Terry Rattue)

Viscount 831 G-ASED has some ancient history at Gatwick, as back in 1959 it was operated by Sudan Airways as ST-AAN for its weekly Gatwick–Khartoum 'Blue Nile' schedule. Bought from BUA by British Midland Airways in February 1967, it is seen here in June 1970 parked on the north finger. BMA flew a total of twenty-four different Viscounts, Series 700s and 800s, for an incredible twenty-one years between 1967 and 1988, and a few of them were still appearing at Gatwick as late as 1985. (Author's collection)

Treffield Aviation, an acronym derived from the founders' names, Lord Trefgarne and Charles Masefield, was set up at Sywell in Northampton in 1965 with two Ansons flying freight charters. After IT contracts were awarded for the 1967 season, Treffield switched to passenger operations and leased two Viscounts from Channel Airways for holiday flights from Gatwick, Cardiff, Bristol and Liverpool. Britannia 102 G-ANBM was leased from Laker that spring and made its first service from Gatwick to Venice on 1 May. Poor weather and aircraft unserviceability led to diversions and angry stranded passengers that summer, and the subsequent bad publicity caused the contracts to be cancelled; Treffield folded in June. (Jacques Guillem collection)

From 1967, getting from Gatwick to Heathrow by public transport was restricted to the Green Line bus that also stopped at Luton Airport, but this was far from ideal and the airlines were demanding a much quicker method. British Westpoint Airlines was first to suggest an air service in 1966, but the airline's closure led to the plans being abandoned. However, in 1969 Cornwall-based Westward Airways declared that it could provide the service with its BN Islander aircraft, and the airport operator, British Airports Authority (BAA), agreed to the idea. Six times daily 'Westward Shuttle' services commenced on 25 June 1969 using BN-2 G-AXFC, supported by a second Islander, G-AXHE. Cost was £4 each way for the fifteen-minute trip. Westward also flew a Newquay–Plymouth–Gatwick–Heathrow schedule and Gatwick–Plymouth–Newquay–Isles of Scilly. Westward withdrew from the route in July 1970 and it was taken over by Southend Air Taxis, but the latter also suffered from high airport charges and packed up the following month. The final London Heathrow–London Gatwick air service was the BAA Airlink, using a twenty-eight-seater S.61 helicopter from 1978 until 1986; each way was £12. (Author's collection)

De Havilland Dove 1B G-ANMJ is seen here on 21 August still wearing Hawker Siddeley Aviation colours. It was leased by Cardinal Airways for passenger and freight charters from Shackleton Aviation in June 1967 after Cardinal's first Dove, G-ALCU, was damaged in a wheels-up landing at Le Mans. Gatwick-based Cardinal was associated with Crushman Air Travel Ltd and both titles appear alongside its movements in the tower logbooks. The company ceased trading in July 1968. (Peter Keating via Tony Eastwood collection)

Bristol 170 Freighter Mk.31 G-APLH is seen here on Gatwick's North Park on 19 June 1965, having performed a round-trip to Tours a day earlier. It was the only new aircraft ever acquired by Dan-Air London. Bought in March 1958, it served alongside two other Bristol Freighters as a reliable workhorse until sold to Lambair in Canada as CF-YDP in 1968. This 'Biffo' was written off after the starboard undercarriage leg collapsed on landing at Christopher Island, Baker Lake, Northern Territories, in June 1970. Just visible behind are the tailfins of a couple of rare visitors to Gatwick, three RAF Vickers Varsitys (WL634, WL627 and WF331) that arrived that day. (Adrian Balch collection)

Gatwick in the 1960s and '70s was a favourite stop-off for various aircraft on delivery flights clearing customs prior to the crossing to Europe. This Shorts Skyvan Series 3 9M-AQG passed through on its way to Malaysia from Belfast on 16 September 1971. Malaysia Air Charter (MAC) started flying in 1962 with a single Cessna 310, and in February 1970, after eight years of services, it applied to operate rural air services using an eighteen-passenger Shorts Skyvan. It borrowed one for trials that month and said that, subject to approvals, it could start in September. Although 9M-AQG arrived over a year later, it was a success and MAC went on to operate seven more Skyvans. (John Crawford)

Now here is a notable aircraft in Gatwick's history. Percival Prince Series 4B G-AMKX was possibly the first aircraft to touch down at the new Gatwick Airport on Thursday, 17 April 1958. Operated by the Ministry of Transport and Civil Aviation, it was carrying out navigation aid/radar calibration duties for the new airport prior to the official opening. Sadly, the available documents fail to say if it actually landed or just carried out approaches and overshoots, so there is some doubt to the story. G-AMKX was one of three Princes built at Luton especially for air calibration duties. The ministry also used a larger President aircraft, G-APMO, which was also seen at Gatwick. The fleet was based at Stansted and later operated HS748s. (Peter Keating)

The view from the spectators' decks at Gatwick in the 1960s was one of the best for catching shots like this. About to taxi out for a flight to Palma in the summer of 1967, Britannia 312 EC-BFK *Mediterraneo* of Air Spain often made three round trips to Spain from Gatwick in a single day. First delivered to BOAC in 1957, this aircraft was bought by Air Spain in 1966 and survived in service until 1972. Air Spain was formed in 1966 and started flying training later that year with the first of two Britannias acquired from British Eagle. While most Spanish charter airlines were still using piston-powered airliners, Air Spain's use of this mighty turboprop gave it an advantage, as it could fly from Helsinki to the Balearic and Canary Islands nonstop with a full load. Air Spain Britannias were occasionally used to fly in Spanish tomatoes during the quieter winter months. (Author's collection)

About to touch down on Runway 26 in April 1968 is British United Airways' Bristol Britannia 307 G-ANCE. Back in the summer of 1960, two of the industry's major players, Airwork and Hunting-Clan, took on the might of BEA and BOAC when they persuaded a group of small UK air companies to join them to create British United Airways. Air Charter, Airwork Helicopters, Bristow Helicopters, Morton Air Services, Olley Air Service and Transair combined to provide a Gatwick-based front-line fleet that consisted of Britannias, Viscounts, DC-3s, DC-6As and DC-4s. Channel Air Bridge, a BUA company, continued to operate under its own name on its cross-Channel car ferry services from Southend. Freddie Laker became the managing director of BUA, backed by some major shipping companies including P&O and British & Commonwealth. After ten busy years, BUA was taken over by Caledonian in 1970, to become Caledonian/BUA and later British Caledonian Airways. (Adrian Balch)

V.808 Viscount G-BBDK was purchased by Castle Donington-based freight airline Air Bridge Carriers (ABC) on 11 April 1974 from Overseas Aero Leasing. It carries the colour scheme of a previous operator, Geneva-based Société Anonyme de Transport Aérien (SATA), which had used this very aircraft when it was HB-ILR on a service to Gatwick back in November 1969. In February 1975, ABC modified this, its only Viscount, to a convertible passenger/freight configuration and leased it to Dan-Air the following month in full passenger configuration to operate its coach-air Lydd to Beauvais schedule. By the time this shot was taken in October 1976, G-BBDK was back with ABC as a freighter; note the windows are protected by internal covers. The aircraft ended its days in a wheels-up landing at Belfast in 1996 while operated by British World Airways. (Bernard King)

The clothing company Junex of Sweden was incorporated in the UK in July 1960 and had its showroom at Park Lane in London. It made men's coats and jackets that are still sought after today. This Anson was originally with the RAF (as TX213) and was civilianised from the RAF Southern Communications Squadron at Bovingdon in 1968 as G-AWRS with Hewitts Investments Co. Ltd, which flew it to Gatwick on 27 August 1969. It was bought by Junex as an executive transport in February 1970 and was photographed at that time at Gatwick. The aircraft later spent time on aerial surveys until it was grounded, and it is now displayed at the North East Land Sea and Air Museum in Sunderland. (Ken Fielding)

Wearing a modified version of its previous Jersey Airlines livery is Handley Page Dart Herald 201 G-APWF. The first of six Jersey Airlines Heralds acquired by British United (Channel Islands) Airways when Jersey Airlines joined the BUA brand in 1962, *Whisky Foxtrot* remained in service until 1981, having carried titles from British United Island Airways (BUIA), British Island Airways (BIA) and Air UK. It carried BUA titles until BUIA was formed in 1968, when BU(CI)A joined up with BUA(Manx) and Morton Air Services. Sorry it's a bit complicated, but that's the airline business for you! (Martin Fenner collection)

Exeter-based South West Aviation Ltd was formed in 1966 with a single Piper Aztec. This Skyvan 2 G-ATPF was leased from the manufacturers Short Brothers and Harland Ltd in early 1968 for passenger and freight charters from Exeter and Bristol. It is seen here at Gatwick that spring, but was returned to Shorts in January 1969 after South West had bought Skyvan Series 3 G-AWCS, which also made an appearance at Gatwick on 10 July 1968. South West was bought out by Ashford airline Air Freight in 1972. G-ATPF was no stranger to Gatwick, having visited in Emerald Airways titles in 1966 and Aeralpi titles in 1967. The aircraft was retired in 1973. (Author's collection)

Europe Aero Service (EAS) was formed in July 1965 as a subsidiary of Société Aero-Sahara with a fleet of Vickers Vikings based at Perpignan in the south of France. Two HP Heralds were bought from failed Swiss airline Globeair in 1968, and they made several visits to London Gatwick. A fleet of fifteen Vickers Vanguards, thirteen bought from Air Canada, commenced services for EAS in April 1972, although some of them went straight to Perpignan for use as spare parts. Two EAS Vanguards, F-BYCE and F-BYCF, were former British Airways Merchantmen freighters with large forward freight doors. A total of eight EAS Vanguards visited Gatwick from 1972 onwards, with F-BVUY making its first visit in May 1976. (Bernard King)

Back in the 1960s, it was possible for anyone to visit the south side maintenance area and photograph whatever was parked outside without attracting the attention of a security guard (there weren't any) or being whisked off to the police station accused of being a terrorist. Previously known as Air Links until 1965, Transglobe Airways came into being on 1 August 1965 after the Bolton Steamship Company had invested sufficiently in the airline to finance the purchase of two Canadian Pacific Britannias. These aircraft replaced the airline's Canadair Argonauts, and with the purchase of series 302 Britannia G-ANCC from Mexico in May 1966 the 'Brits' commenced social group charters to Canada and the USA, and holiday charter flights to the Mediterranean and beyond. This nice view of Transglobe's Bristol Britannia 302 G-ANCC was taken in July 1969 in the maintenance area, where it had been in storage since Transglobe had folded in November 1968. It was sold that year to International Aviation Services (IAS), which, at the time, was managing African Safari Airways, and it planned to use it as a spares source for 5X-UVH. IAS never needed it, though, and it ferried to Biggin Hill in March 1970, where it was later scrapped. (Author's collection)

A very special Viscount! BEA's V806 Viscount G-APIM is seen about to depart for the Channel Islands sometime in 1970. In August 1984, it was given the name *Viscount Stephen Piercey* by its then owners, British Air Ferries, in memory of Stephen who had been killed in a mid-air collision while on a photo mission for *Flight International* magazine. After it was seriously damaged at Southend by a runaway Shorts 330 in January 1988, it was used for spares reclamation until rescued by the Brooklands Museum, where it has been beautifully restored and now takes pride of place alongside other Vickers airliners, VC10, Vanguard and Viking. The author has been involved with fundraising for this aircraft since its arrival at Brooklands and The Friends of Viscount Stephen Piercey and the Viscount Team at Brooklands still look after it to this day. (Bob Wall collection)

This 1944-built de Havilland Dragon Rapide G-AHKU was once operated by BOAC and then BEA, whose colours can still be seen on it in this photograph where it is parked by the north finger in August 1968. By then it was owned by Bryan Neely, proprietor of Land's End-based Scillonia Airways, but it only remained airworthy for another couple of years as its Certificate of Airworthiness expired in August 1970, by which time Scillonia had ceased flying. It was eventually withdrawn from use in 1972, never to fly again. (Author's collection)

In February 1946, British airline Silver City Airways registered a partner airline in Paris to 'legalise' and protect the French end of its cross-Channel car ferry operations. Fully financed by Silver City, it was named Société Commerciale Aérienne du Littoral (SCAL) and was operated by the Le Touquet Airport Authority under Monsieur J.H. Sansard. Note that SCAL had the same initials as Silver City. A few Bristol 170 Freighters were registered in their name, but it is thought only Mk.31 F-BFUO ever came to Gatwick, with at least twenty-nine visits recorded between March 1960 and September 1966. SCAL bought it from Aer Lingus in October 1956 and sold it to Aer Turas on 21 November 1966. (Author's collection)

Formed in 1970, British Island Airways could trace its lineage back to Silver City Airways, Jersey Airlines, British United (Channel Islands) Airways and lastly British United Island Airways. When BUA joined up with Caledonian that year, BIA remained under the control of the British and Commonwealth Shipping Group and adopted this orange scheme. BIA Heralds (G-APWE seen here) were mainly used for passenger flights from Gatwick to the Channel Islands, although they also flew a Gatwick to Antwerp service in conjunction with SABENA and a service to Manchester on behalf of British Caledonian. They also flew to the Channel Islands from Southampton, and from other UK airports, and several Heralds were based at Blackpool. In 1980, BIA merged with Air Anglia to become Air UK, and in 1982 a new BIA was formed at Gatwick with BAC 1-11s to operate holiday charter flights. (Author's collection)

Parked on Stand 1 at Gatwick on 23 July 1965 is de Havilland Devon VP955, carrying the title Royal Air Force Transport Command, although the sun's reflection masks some of it. It arrived from RAF Northolt using the radio call sign GWA51 and returned there the same day. Note the immaculate Grumman Mallard amphibian G-ASCS belonging to Ferranti that arrived that day from Valley in North Wales. Upon RAF retirement, VP955 was sold in the UK as G-BLPD, but that registration was not used and it became G-DVON with the Staverton-based '955 Preservation Group' in 1984. They flew it at air shows for many years, but by 2000 it was in store at Kemble, and by 2015 it was noted dismantled at Calcutt near Cricklade, Wiltshire, alongside sister ship XA880. (Peter Marson)

Awaiting its next load of passengers for Jersey in April 1972, BEA's Viscount 802 G-AOHJ carries the large Channel Islands titles worn by the Viscounts of that division. The world's first turboprop airliner to enter commercial service, the Viscount was a regular sight at Gatwick from the first day that it opened in 1958 (Transair) until the last visits of the type with British World Airlines around 1997. G-AOHJ first visited Gatwick in December 1958 in full BEA colours, and after retirement from the national airline in 1976, it was flown to Newcastle, where it was scrapped. (Bob Wall collection)

This immaculate de Havilland Dove 1 G-AJOS was part of a fleet of mostly Doves and Herons belonging to Coventry-based Executive Air Transport (EAT) that operated for a dozen years from 1961. EAT flew DC-3 Dakota G-ANEG on a series of schedules, but most flights were in Doves and Herons under charter. EAT's experience with these DH types prompted it to set up Executive Air Engineering at Coventry, and this became a major force in the repair and maintenance of these aircraft. G-AJOS was flown in full EAT colours on charters from Coventry and Birmingham for four years and was seen at Gatwick on 4 July 1968. (Peter Keating via Tony Eastwood collection)

Showing off its Paris Air Show number at Gatwick in June 1973, Short Skyvan G-AZRY was photographed outside the General Aviation Terminal on its way home from the show, which became infamous for the tragic crash of the Tupolev Tu-144 there. First flown at Belfast in May 1972, G-AZRY was used as a demonstrator by Shorts and made its first visit to Gatwick on 20 July 1972. It was later given Braathens and Air Executive Norway titles whilst performing proving and demonstration flights. It was sold in Norway, not to Braathens, but to Busy Bee in July 1973, becoming LN-NPA. In 2018, the aircraft was still operational, flying for Pink Aviation Services in Austria as OE-FDK. (Author's collection)

Parked outside the General Aviation Terminal in August 1972 is de Havilland Dove G-ANUT of the Civil Aviation Flying Unit. Based at Stansted, its fleet of Doves, Princes and Presidents were regular visitors to Gatwick right from the start in 1958. The fleet, initially operated by the Ministry of Transport and Civil Aviation, flew all over the UK and sometimes abroad, mostly in connection with airport navigational aid calibration. The variety of tasks flown included flight-testing pilots for commercial licences, instrument ratings and instructor ratings, as well as flights where they would be controlled by trainee air traffic controllers at the College of Air Traffic Control at Hurn Airport. (Tony Merton Jones)

Morton Air Services, DH Herons were a regular sight at Gatwick from late 1959 when the airline's operations switched from Croydon to Gatwick, the Morton name only disappearing when it was absorbed into BUA in 1968. This Heron, G-AOXL, has a claim to fame: on 30 September 1959, the last day of Croydon Airport operations, it flew the last scheduled service from the airport when it departed to Rotterdam at 1838, appropriately commanded by Captain Last. It flew back to Gatwick the following day. To commemorate this event, a non-flying Heron registered G-ANUO was painted up as G-AOXL and displayed on poles outside the Croydon Airport terminal in November 1996. (Author's collection)

Parked on Stand 2 at Gatwick on a quiet Sunday in May 1960, North-South Airlines' passenger version Bristol Freighter Mk. 21 G-AHJD was a very early example of this sturdy workhorse, having first flown in 1946. North-South, which also operated DH Herons and DC-3s, was based in Leeds/Bradford at Yeadon airfield, but after it acquired G-AHJD in April 1960, it was leased to Air Condor at Southend for a few months, returning to Leeds for North-South services at the weekend. On this Gatwick visit it had arrived from Heathrow early in the morning and then made a return trip to Rotterdam. (Jacques Guillem collection)

Two series 102 Bristol Britannias that were once flown by Laker Airways at Gatwick were bought from National Aero Leasing by Indonesian Angkasa Civil Air Transport in February 1969. The old Laker colour scheme was painted over in green and gold at Gatwick and both aircraft (PK-ICA and ICB) were delivered to Jakarta. Their use is not confirmed, but most probably they flew pilgrims to Mecca for the Hadj. The following year, the same airline leased an ex-Air Canada Vickers Vanguard as PK-ICC. The Britannias were both scrapped at Jakarta in December 1971. (Author's collection)

This Avro 748 Series 2 G-ATMI first appeared at Gatwick in Autair colours in April 1966. Owned by Court Line Aviation (successor to Autair) in 1971, it was one of a pair leased to Southend-based British Air Ferries (BAF) in 1971, during which time it was fully painted in BAF colours and usually flown on its routes from Southend to Ostend and Le Touquet. Bought by Dan-Air London in 1975, this well-travelled 748, often fondly referred to as a 'Budgie', also flew for British Airways and was finally grounded at Blackpool in 1999. The Avro/BAe748 was a British success story, with 382 sold to eighty operators in fifty countries. (Author's collection)

Inscribed with the title IAS Cargo Airlines, this freight-door equipped Series 312F Britannia G-AOVF had many thousands of miles under its wings, having previously flown front-line passenger services with BOAC as a Series 312 from 1958 to 1964; then followed four years with British Eagle before it was given a freight door in 1968, making it a 312F. Spells with Donaldson and African Safari followed before International Aviation Services bought the aircraft in 1972. Seen here in March 1977, G-AOVF has survived into preservation. Since 1984 it has been displayed at RAF Cosford, initially in BOAC colours but now in RAF markings. (Author's collection)

In February 1962, Eros Airlines (UK) Ltd announced it would commence IT charters from Gatwick using a fleet of three Vickers Vikings acquired from the liquidator of Air Safaris. Eros took over the offices of Falcon Airways in the Gatwick terminal and flew its first service at the end of March. After a busy summer, problems with the ATLB regarding the 1963 season saw the fleet diminish to two Vikings, G-AHOW and G-AJBX. Eros became the last Gatwick-based airline to operate Vikings and finally died in the spring of 1964. Note the iconic Hangar 4 behind, built of wood for Overseas Aviation in 1960; the author watched it burn down in 1991. (Chris Knott collection)

2
DAKOTAS

What is the world's most iconic classic airliner? There can be only one answer, the Douglas DC-3 Dakota, usually known in the USA as the C-47 Skytrain. First flown in 1935, the 'Dak' went on to serve in pretty much every theatre of war during the Second World War, and when hundreds were civilianised post war, it became the most numerous airliner in commercial operations worldwide. Around 10,000 military C-47s were built by Douglas and the aircraft was also built under licence in Russia and Japan. The pre-1958 Gatwick saw Dakotas parked alongside the Beehive terminal, while on the official day of opening in 1958, BEA's Dakota (called 'Pionair' by BEA) G-ALXK took off on a passenger charter to Jersey. The first few years of the new Gatwick saw dozens of Dakotas in service with British airlines, having the Channel Islands as their prime destination. Used by several major airlines for flights to the new Gatwick throughout the 1960s, this remarkable aircraft was still visiting Gatwick in the twenty-first century, with the occasional flight by Coventry-based Air Atlantique.

One of the earliest colour shots found for this book, this view looking south from the terminal in 1960 shows an impressive line-up of classic 'propliners'. Nearest the camera is one of Transair's Douglas DC-3 Dakotas, G-AOUD. Also visible are two Air Safaris Vikings and a couple of BEA Dakotas, while over at the maintenance area are three Vikings, two DC-3s and two Viscounts. Transair operated up to twenty DC-3s in the period October 1952 to July 1960. G-AOUD was sold in Miami as N4848 in 1969, but had been scrapped by the end of 1970. (Author's collection)

Parked up near the freight sheds in January 1976 is Skyways Cargo Airlines' Douglas C-47B Dakota G-AMWW. The aircraft was used for the nightly freight service to Amsterdam, flown on behalf of KLM. The author sampled one of these trips in early 1978, flying out in G-APBC on 31 January and returning to Lydd in G-AMWW (a bad move due to poor public transport in Kent!) on 7 February. Based at Lydd Airport from October 1974, Air Freight Ltd was operating Europe's largest Dakota fleet (seven) from 1975 when a major company reorganisation changed the name to Skyways Cargo Airline. (John Crawford)

Spartan's C-47A CF-ICU was used for aerial survey work in many countries and made its first recorded visit to Gatwick in June 1960, routing Rome–Gatwick–Prestwick–Keflavik–Sondrestrom–Frosbisher–Ottawa on its way back home from surveying the Mekong river at Vientiane. Seen here in April 1963, it carries the titles 'Kenya Canada Commonwealth Africa Programme' on the nose. This was an integrated forestry survey programme based in Mombasa. It had arrived from Rome on 25 February, made a local flight on 1 March and then, rather than flying back to Ottawa, it sat around at Air Couriers for a year before flying off to Canada via Prestwick on 18 February 1964. (Author's collection)

The usual airfield works in the centre of the airport look very quiet in this frosty December 1969 shot of Welltrade C-47B N3179Q. Previously serving with the Royal Air Force and the German Air Force, Dakota N3179Q was acquired by Shannon-based Welltrade Inc. in November 1969 for gas and oilfield support flights. Welltrade, which also owned a Cherokee and an Aztec, went into joint operations with Moormanair at Amsterdam in late 1970, and the Dakota became PH-MOA. It was written off in June 1971 in a non-fatal landing accident at Southend, carrying a load of Dutch football supporters. (Bob Wall)

Another one-off Dakota visitor to Gatwick was this Lebanese-registered example, OD-AEP. It arrived from Nice on 5 May 1966 and departed the next day to Stansted. Carrying Pan American Indonesia Oil Co. titles with an additional 'On Charter to L.A.T.' inscription (LAT was Lebanese Air Transport), it was reportedly leased to Pan American Indonesia Oil Co. from April 1965 for a year by British United (CI) Airways, where it had been registered G-ANEG. After overhaul, the aircraft left Stansted on 21 October 1966 bound for Nice and the Middle East, serving with Gulf Aviation again as G-ANEG for services in Bahrain. One pilot recalled that it was 'knackered' after flying around Oman with fresh fruit and meat … It was still dumped at Bahrain in 1982. (Terry Rattue)

Morton Air Services moved down from Croydon to Gatwick in 1959 and commenced schedules to Rotterdam, Swansea and the Channel Islands with its fleet of Rapides, Doves and Herons. In 1962, British United Airways transferred three Dakotas (G-AMHJ, MRA and MSV) to Morton, initially for freight charters. The illustrated G-AMYJ joined the fleet in late 1965 from British United (Channel Islands) Airways and commenced Morton services with a Gatwick to Southend hop on 9 January 1966, prior to flying a series of Ford tractor parts charters from Southend to Antwerp. When the Morton name disappeared in the BUA empire in November 1968, G-AMYJ was sold to South West Aviation. (Jacques Guillem collection)

This Liberian-registered 1943-built Douglas C-53D Skytrooper, EL-AAZ, was delivered to Africa through Heathrow in April 1955 after sale by Pan American Airways. It reportedly carried the name *Monrovia Star* when it was seen at Gatwick on 26–27 May 1968 (arriving from Madrid, and departing to Malmö), but there is no sign of an external name in this photo. The aircraft flew services between Monrovia and Freetown, and when Liberian National Airlines merged with Ducor Air Transport in 1974 to become Air Liberia, this aircraft was still in service, and it remained so until 1976 when it was sold to Ethiopian Airlines. This Dakota has a small claim to fame in that it features in a short video on YouTube. (Author's collection)

The two Turkish Airlines Dakotas, TC-YUK and TC-YOL, were pretty regular visitors to Gatwick on charter flights from 1961 to 1967, mixed in with visits by THY Viscounts. They appear to have routed via Rome to Istanbul, although the scheduled flights to Heathrow in 1961 flew Ankara–Istanbul–Vienna–Frankfurt–London. TC-YOL is seen here on Wednesday, 22 September 1965 parked up on the north side, waiting for its return flight three days later. The first ever visit to Gatwick by THY never actually landed. Viscount TC-SEV was diverted from Heathrow in poor weather in February 1959 and crashed into Russ Hill on approach, killing fourteen of the twenty-four occupants aboard. (Mike Axe collection)

C-47B G-AMPO is seen here at Gatwick in November 1972, shortly after Macedonian Aviation, a subsidiary of Macedonian Securities, began passenger and charter operations from a base at Southend, having received a period of training support by Dan-Air. It famously flew a dramatic rescue mission to Beirut via Genoa and Brindisi in September 1972, when it departed Gatwick flown by Macedonian's Captain Harry Chang to rescue twenty-five wedding guests stranded at Beirut Airport, which was being besieged by the Israeli Air Force in retaliation for the murder of Israeli athletes by Palestinian terrorists at the Munich Olympics. Escorted by Israeli aircraft, Harry landed G-AMPO on a taxiway at Beirut and, without shutting down, swiftly loaded the passengers and took off for Cyprus, where the wedding party continued. G-AMPO returned safely to Gatwick a couple of days later. Macedonian Aviation stopped flying in November 1974. (John Crawford)

One of nine Douglas Dakotas flown by Jersey Airlines from 1959, until it evolved into British United (Channel Islands) Airways in 1963, C-47B G-AMZG is seen here in its original Transair colour scheme, but with Jersey Airlines titles at Gatwick around 1962. G-AMZG was one of many in the fleet that were actually owned by the Alares Development Co. Ltd in Jersey. The Dakotas flew mostly on the busy tourist routes from Gatwick, Southampton and Bournemouth to Jersey, together with services to northern France. Interestingly, Jersey Airlines leased Middle East Airlines Viscount OD-ACU to fly LGW-JER schedules for the whole of July 1961, due to the late delivery of new Heralds. (Chris Knott collection)

Irelfly started operations from Shoreham and Gatwick in February 1966 with a single Dakota (G-AMPY) leased from Aviation Overhauls. Some handsome extra revenue was generated flying freight during the national seamen's strike in May and June that year, prompting Irelfly to acquire two more, G-ALYF and G-AMSH. All three Dakotas were then flown on ad-hoc passenger and freight charters, but the pace of work slackened once the ships were sailing again. The company planned to acquire Viscount 700s for use on IT charters from Bristol and Cardiff during the 1967 summer season, but by November 1966 Irelfly was in financial trouble and ceased flying. G-AMSH is seen here on its first visit to Gatwick on 13 July 1966 after arriving from Liverpool. (Tony Clarke collection)

Taxying onto stand on the North Pier at Gatwick on the afternoon of 22 May 1967 is Faroe Airways' flight KK631, Douglas C-47A OY-DMN. It arrived on a passenger charter from Groningen in the Netherlands and remained at London Gatwick until the evening of the 27th, when it flew back to Groningen as KK422. The Faroes, a group of eighteen islands halfway between Scotland and Iceland, are a province of Denmark with aircraft carrying Danish OY registrations. Faroe Airways began services with a de Havilland Heron in 1964, and in 1965 this former Linjeflyg and SAS DC-3 joined the fleet after a repaint at Copenhagen. The tail logo is a Viking Helmet with 'FA' inscribed. OY-DMN made only one visit to Gatwick; usually it flew a regular service between Vagar and Copenhagen via Kirkwall in the Orkneys. Operations ceased late in September 1967, and this 1942 vintage Dakota was broken up at Kastrup, Demark, the following year. Faroes–Gatwick services were most recently operated by the current Faroes national carrier, Atlantic Airways, for a short period in the 2010s, using an Airbus A319. (Author's collection)

A very rare visitor in August 1975 was this 1944-vintage C-47A N24320 of Evergreen. Captained by Skip Alderson, it was on its way to Niger in Africa to spray bugs on behalf of the United Nations, an arduous thirteen-day trip with seventy-two hours in the air. It returned to the USA and amazingly it is still there, preserved at the Museum of Mountain Flying in Missoula, Montana. Its continued existence is both surprising and poignant as it survived a ditching in the Monongahela River on 22 December 1954 on approach to Pittsburgh-Allegheny County Airport. In this tragedy, ten of the twenty-eight occupants lost their lives in an accident attributed to fuel exhaustion – the aircraft had been flying a Johnson Flying Service charter from Newark to Tacoma. Prior to this in 1949, N24320 dropped a party of fifteen parachuting smoke jumpers on a fire 20 miles north of Helena, Montana. Tragically, twelve were killed in the blaze, which made national news as the 'Mann Gulch fire'. In view of its history, this aircraft now carries memorial status. (John Crawford)

Regular services to Gatwick by Spanish national airline Iberia Douglas DC-4s commenced in 1961, followed by its magnificent Lockheed Super Constellations from 1962 to 1965, serving Palma, Barcelona, Valencia and Malaga. This appears to be the only ever visit of an Iberia C-47 to Gatwick. It arrived from Glasgow on 30 October 1965 and departed to Bordeaux. EC-ASF joined Iberia on 10 October 1963; it was then sold to the Spanish Air Force in 1966, which flew it until it became N1350M in October 1981. It is now preserved at Frankfurt Airport in United States Air Force (USAF) Second World War colours as 43-49081 *The Berlin Train*, in memory of the Berlin Airlift. (Author's collection)

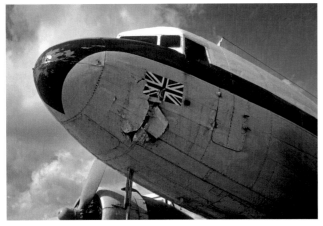

Former Gibraltar-based Gibair Douglas C-47A Dakota G-AMFV was sold to Biggin Hill-based Fairflight Charters Ltd in June 1970, although it was officially registered to C47 Aviation Ltd. In company with the airline's three DH Doves (more were acquired later), the 'Dak' flew several charters from Gatwick, including one that took a live dolphin to Majorca. Early work also saw the aircraft hauling cargo during a dock strike in July 1970. In August 1970, it disgraced itself when an undercarriage leg collapsed while turning on to stand, causing the No. 1 propeller to break off and slice into the side of the cockpit, just missing the captain's foot. The nose was patched up by Dan-Air and a spare wing from G-AMPP and a new engine were fitted before it was flown to Lasham for repairs involving a chunk of nose from G-AMSU. (Above author's collection; left Bob Wall)

Disembarking onto a windy ramp next to the North Pier at Gatwick is Antwerp-based Delta Air Transport's 1942-vintage C-47B OO-VDF. This was a rare sight at Gatwick, with just this single recorded visit on 1 May 1968, as Delta tended to use Southend for its UK flights. Note the Caledonian ground hostess giving out some documents and the white-hatted customs man waiting to get aboard. Delta Air Transport was formed in 1966 for air-taxi and general charters using Cessna light aircraft, but once it acquired DC-3s (OO-VDF was bought in December 1967 and lasted until 1972) the company became increasingly popular and commenced scheduled services on behalf of KLM. The airline later acquired DC-6s, Convair 440s, FH-227s and eventually pure jets, before evolving into SN Brussels Airlines in 2002. (Jacques Guillem collection)

A quiet period finds British United Island Airways Freighter C-47Bs G-AMSV and G-AMHJ in the maintenance area in March 1969. Together with G-AMRA, they formed the all-cargo fleet of British Island Airways in 1970, sporting the distinctive orange livery. This fleet was mainly used on the early-morning newspaper runs to Hanover, Düsseldorf and the Channel Islands. Built in 1944, G-AMSV joined the RAF as a Dakota IV in 1945 and served for seven years before becoming G-AMSV, initially with Air Service Training Ltd at Hamble. In February 2018 it was gifted to the Indian Air Force Vintage Flight. (Chris England)

Ethiopian Air Force Douglas C-47 '707' must have really wowed the local plane spotters when it turned up at Gatwick on 7 March 1962. The arrival of such an exotic machine was what every enthusiast dreamed of, although those who were only interested in civilian aircraft probably dismissed it! It is interesting that even after more than fifty years, the previous identities of this aircraft are unknown. The Ethiopian Air Force reportedly operated a dozen C-47s, serial numbers 701 to 712, but the origins of only a few have been traced – a real mystery ship. (Jack Friell via Steve Hill)

Exeter-based South West Aviation Ltd was formed in 1966, initially using light twin-prop aircraft. A Skyvan Series 2 was leased for freight charters early in 1968, before a new Skyvan Series 3 and this Douglas C-47B Dakota G-APBC joined the fleet that summer. It was chartered by Mortons at Gatwick for several weeks of newspaper services in 1968 and is seen here the following summer. The company went into voluntary liquidation in February 1972, but continued to fly its two Dakotas until later that year, when G-APBC was sold to Air Freight at Lydd. (David Howell collection)

A very grand airline name on a pretty ordinary Dakota that managed never to operate a revenue service! International Air Cargo (IAC) was formed in Guernsey in 1966 to operate freight charters from Guernsey to northern France, southern Ireland and southern England with two Dakotas. This aircraft, G-ATBE, was the only one to appear in IAC livery and it appears to have flown very little. Having arrived from Luton on 26 May 1967, it flew that evening to Ostend before returning the following morning. It left for Luton en route to Prestwick for overhaul by SAL on 3 June, having been purchased by Handley Page for use as a support aircraft during the Jetstream's overseas flight trials, and was never seen at Gatwick again. (Author's collection)

This 1945-vintage Douglas C-47D Dakota GR+106 had previously served with the RAF and the USAF. Released to the West German Air Force under the Military Assistance Programme (MAP) in 1956, in December 1959 it was transferred to the transport 'reserve', thanks to the arrival of the Nord Noratlas into German service. It was being operated by 1./LTG 61 at Neubiberg when it appeared at Gatwick on 5 September 1960. After making a local flight on the 9th, it returned to Germany. Its post-military service was with Bechtel Corp in Abu Dhabi and Arax Airlines in Nigeria. (Jack Friell via Steve Hill)

Despite the creation of British United Airways in the summer of 1960, this C-53 version of the Dakota remained registered to Silver City right through until 1971. Converted by Air Couriers to a radio calibration aircraft and named *City of Canterbury*, in November 1960 it departed on a five-year Ministry of Aviation calibration contract to Cyprus, Bahrain, Lagos, Kano and Accra. In 1969 it completed more than 600 hours of calibration flying. In February 1970 the Radio Calibration Unit (RCU) was awarded a two-year contract for work in Saudi Arabia and the Gulf. Manned by a crew of five, G-AOBN travelled extensively, checking navigational aids. It later became part of the BUIA fleet and carried its titles. It returned to freighter configuration and went to Air Anglia and later Air Freight before departing to Ethiopia in July 1977, where it was destroyed on the ground during an air raid the following month. (Chris Knott collection)

The stylish zigzag cheatline of the Royal Canadian Air Force always suited its C-47 Dakotas. KN291, seen here on 4 August 1968, also carries the title 1 Air Division, which was established to meet Canada's NATO air defence commitments in Europe with fighters and transports. The title and the Royal Canadian Air Force (RCAF) wording would change that year as the three Canadian military forces amalgamated and 1 Air Division was replaced by No. 1 Canadian Air Group. The RCAF had over seventy C-47s, with this one coming from RAF stocks and retaining its RAF serial. It later became CF-BKW in Canada, then HK-2665 in Colombia, where it was impounded in the mid-1990s carrying a fake registration PT-JAS. Note the Decca Navigator Ambassador G-ALZP and a BUA Herald taxying out to the western holding point. (Author's collection)

On final approach for runway 09 on 16 June 1973 is British Island Airways Air Cargo C-47B G-AMRA. This was one of three Dakotas (the others were G-AMHJ and G-AMSV) that changed from the BUIA Freighter livery to adopt the smart orange BIA scheme in the summer of 1970. The Dakotas plied their trade mostly between Bournemouth, Gatwick, Düsseldorf, Hanover and the Channel Islands, until 30 May 1974 when the last BIA DC-3 flight brought a cargo of flowers from Guernsey to Bournemouth before positioning empty to Gatwick. In 2018, G-AMRA was awaiting German registry with Air Service Berlin. (Peter Guiver)

Dan-Air Services was registered as an airline in May 1953. A subsidiary of Davies and Newman Ltd, a London-based shipping broker, Dan-Air acquired its first aircraft, Douglas C-47B Dakota G-AMSU, the following month and commenced IT services from its base at Southend to Calvi in Corsica; it also flew a handful of emigrant services to South Africa. Seen here in July 1966, *Sierra Uniform* stayed in the fleet until 1968. It was later scrapped at Lasham in Hampshire, but as it had been Dan-Air's first aircraft, it was commemorated when Dan-Air's C-47 G-AMPP was painted up as G-AMSU and preserved outside the Dan-Air maintenance hangar at the Lasham base, where it proudly remained until 1991. (Author's collection)

Bought by new Gatwick airline Air Links Ltd from Aer Lingus in 1959, Douglas C-47A Dakota 3 G-APUC was overhauled by Scottish Aviation at Prestwick before entering service on ad-hoc passenger and freight charters from Gatwick. However, its first commercial service was out of Southend on 22 July 1959, having been delivered from Prestwick to Gatwick on 8 July. Seen here in 1962, G-APUC was a regular at Gatwick during 1959, 1960 and 1961, although it had often been based at Lympne for Skyways coach-air work, and Heathrow, operating BEA freight schedules to West Germany. Air Links sold G-APUC in September 1962, and by 1964 it was flying in Nepal as 9N-AAM. (Peter Keating via Tony Eastwood)

3

FOURS, SIXES AND SEVENS

The Douglas Aircraft Company of Santa Monica in California responded to a request from United Air Lines in 1935 for a four-engine long-range airliner. To help with the cost of the prototype, five major US airlines gave $100,000 each to Douglas, which produced a single example of the first DC-4 that had three tail fins and a continuously curving fuselage that looked like a giant DC-3. Complex and expensive, it was abandoned, and a new simplified and smaller DC-4 with a conventional single fin appeared in 1942 as the C-54 Skymaster for US military service. Over 1,200 were built and the type found fame in the Berlin Airlift. Using the same wing as the DC-4, Douglas then built the larger and pressurised DC-6 (military designation C-118), which first flew in 1946. The type was a huge success with airline operators all over the world. Over 700 were built and some are still flying freight in Alaska in 2019. Douglas's last piston-engine airliner was the DC-7, larger and more powerful than the 'Six'; it had turbo-compound engines and could cruise at 355mph (308kts/571kmh). Identifiable by the four-bladed propellers, the DC-7 evolved further into the transatlantic–capable DC-7C with longer wings and more fuel capacity. At the time of writing, three DC-7s are still used as water bombers in Oregon, but these are the only flyers left.

This rare shot at Gatwick was taken by the late Peter Keating, whose job as a purser with BOAC allowed him access to airport ramps around the world, where his high-quality 35mm camera was used to great effect. This Iberia Douglas DC-4 Skymaster EC-AEO was a summer visitor on IT charters to Gatwick from 1961 until 1964, when it was sold to Aviation Traders Ltd at Southend for conversion into an ATL.98 Carvair. It first flew as a Carvair in March 1965 and was delivered to Aviaco in Spain. The small circle at the top of the fin contains the Iberia fleet number 115. (Peter Keating via Tony Eastwood collection)

The very last Douglas DC-6 to be built, DC-6B YU-AFB, belonging to the Yugoslav government, arrived at Gatwick on 3 February 1969, the same day that a Norwegian C-119 made an appearance. The same aircraft had made at least two previous visits, in 1962 and 1965, when it was operated by Adria Airways on its regular holiday flights operated by state-owned Yugotours from and to Zagreb and Ljubljana. YU-AFB served the military and civil airlines in Yugoslavia until 1975, when it was donated along with the second Air Force DC-6B to the Zambian Air Force. They flew them for a couple of years, then parked them for another fifteen years, when they were bought and restored by Namibia Commercial Aviation in 1994. The aircraft was still being stored at Windhoek in 2018, although it is understood that it has been purchased by an American buyer. (Bernard King)

Union de Transports Aériens (UTA) was formed in Paris in October 1963 when two French airlines, TAI and UAT, merged. The combined fleet comprised six DC-8-30s, eight DC-6Bs, two DC-6As, two DC-4s and a Beech 18. Summer charters from Paris (Le Bourget) to Gatwick started in 1965, using DC-6s, including DC-6B F-BGSL pictured here, and carried on until late 1967 when services stopped. UTA evolved into a major airline, but with long routes and few destinations it was expensive to run and on 1 January 1992 it was completely merged into Air France. Note the Luxair Vickers Viscount parked behind. (Jacques Guillem collection)

This immaculate Douglas DC-7C was leased to short-lived US Airways for transatlantic charters in June 1964 and made its first appearance in this anonymous scheme at Gatwick the following month. It had previously visited while operated by Overseas National in 1963. Formed by Captain Lucien Pickett, US Airways also flew Super Constellation N9642Z, which made a few appearances at Gatwick. The DC-7C made at least nine visits under the US Airways banner during the summer of 1964, some of them carrying immigrants from Kenya and Jamaica. It was then sold to Südflug in Germany as D-ABAN. (Niall Booth collection)

Ethiopian Airlines (EAL) had one of the most iconic airline colour schemes ever painted on an airliner. In total, EAL flew a total of five seventy-one-seater Douglas DC-6s, although it would appear that only two, ET-AAX and ET-AAY, visited Gatwick, with AAY first appearing inbound from Belgrade in September 1965 and AAX inbound from Le Bourget in May 1967. EAL initially ordered two new DC-6Bs plus spares in 1956 for US$4 million with an option on a third aircraft. DC-6B ET-AAY, seen here during a rare visit in the summer of 1968, was delivered to EAL brand new in 1958, and thanks to excellent care and attention it continued in service until it was sadly destroyed at Asmara in March 1970, when it overran the runway after landing on a freight flight. It had flown 19,646 flying hours. (Jacques Guillem collection)

Plenty of ramp action here for the spectators on the North Pier as Trans Europa's Douglas DC-7 EC-BBH prepares for another load of holidaymakers bound for the Spanish beaches on 23 August 1970. Trans Europa Compañia de Aviacíon SA was formed in July 1965 to fly from Barcelona to the Spanish resorts. Missing out the usual start-up fleet of DC-3s and DC-4s, Trans Europa started big with the purchase of this DC-7 and only in the following year did it buy DC-4s and DC-7Cs. These 'propliners' were replaced by Caravelles from the summer of 1969, and by the early 1970s this DC-7 and the three DC-7Cs had been grounded. The airline was merged into Iberia in 1979. (Author's collection)

Trans Atlantic's Douglas C-54A (DC-4) N90443 graced the ramp at Gatwick at least twenty-two times in the second half of 1961, mainly undertaking passenger charters in the wake of the Overseas Aviation collapse in August. Trans Atlantic Airlines (TAA) was an American-registered airline founded in March 1961 by Texas-born owner Daniel Hailey Walcott Jr and based at Gatwick with two DC-4s (N90443 and N6531D) and a C-46 (N10435). Despite the name, the airline only operated passenger and freight charters in Europe, Africa and the Middle East. Walcott was later proved to be a smuggler of arms, gold and watches, and spent time in jail in India. One of his DC-4s was impounded at Gatwick after a disagreement about airport fees, and after this was corrected, Walcott moved TAA to Luxembourg. He used Piper Apache N3146P for his personal transport, and this was also a regular at Gatwick prior to the move. Amazingly, N90443 still exists! After being impounded at Brussels in 1963, it was later moved to Overbolare/Geraardsbergen, where it still resides as a plaything for the Phoenix Gliding Club. (Brian Stainer via Tony Eastwood)

A regular visitor between 1961 and 1965 was this Douglas 'Super DC-6B' F-BHEE. Originally delivered to Transports Aériens Intercontinentaux (TAI) in 1955, F-BHEE became part of the huge Union de Transports Aériens (UTA) airline in September 1963 when TAI and Union Aeromaritime de Transport (UAT) merged. It was repainted in much less colourful UTA colours and continued to visit Gatwick, sometimes with two or three rotations a day. TAI and UAT both operated long-haul schedules, principally to the French overseas provinces and the former French colonies, with routes extending far into the Pacific Ocean. It ended its flying days in Southeast Asia with Bird Air, which flew for the US government in Laos. (Jacques Guillem collection)

One of two DC-4 Skymasters (actually C-54s) leased by Dan-Air London from Trans World Leasing in 1965 for passenger and freight work from Gatwick, G-APID (the other was G-ARXJ) was often employed on Inclusive Tours. *India Delta*, like their later DC-7, acquired a nickname, *Rapid Gapid*. Dan-Air flew the aircraft from March 1965 to February 1966, before Invicta leased this old lady, but after a nosewheel collapse at Manston in June 1966, it was stored and eventually sold to Spantax for spare parts in August 1967. Its remains later became the Aerolandia snack bar in Seville, Spain, but this was wrecked in a storm and eventually scrapped. (Author's collection)

An occasional visitor in 1968–69 was this Saudi Arabian Airlines Douglas DC-6A freighter; note the covers to protect the cabin windows. Seen here on 24 June 1968, it had arrived from Bournemouth and stayed until the 28th before returning to Riyadh via Athens. These visits to Bournemouth were to collect equipment and stores connected to the contract held by Bournemouth-based Airwork Services, which was maintaining and running the Royal Saudi Air Force. The port side of the aircraft had two large upward-opening freight doors and the airline titles were written in English. After retirement, it was donated to Yemen Airways as 4W-ABP and was still stored at Sana'a in 1982. (Jacques Guillem collection)

Spanish holidays, particularly to the Balearic Islands, were another staple of Gatwick's initial golden era. Palma de Mallorca-based Spantax was a big player in this market, and a regular visitor to Gatwick from 1963 onwards. A total of eight Douglas DC-7s were flown, including this ex-SABENA DC-7C EC-ATQ, which Spantax acquired in 1964. It was damaged in a hard landing at Madrid Barajas in October 1970, thankfully with no casualties, and it was decided not to repair it. The Spantax DC-7Cs kept appearing right through until the early 1970s, but were gradually replaced by the airline's Convair 990 Coronado jets. Note the light aircraft parked on the grass instead of at the General Aviation Terminal and the British Midland Viscount and RCAF Yukon parked at the end of the North Park. (Left Chris Knott collection; right author's collection)

The Afghanistan state airline Ariana commenced domestic services with a small fleet of DC-3s in 1955 under the name Aryana. From early 1957, Pan American Airways took over the running of the airline and changed its name to Ariana Afghan Airlines. Two DC-4s arrived for international services that year and Ariana's first DC-6A, YA-DAN, was delivered in April 1960, followed by YA-DAO in 1963. These DC-6s flew the 'Marco Polo' route from Kabul to Frankfurt, and from 13 August 1966 this route was extended to Gatwick. This weekly service, FG701 westbound and FG702 eastbound, continued with DC-6s until Ariana acquired its Boeing 727 YA-FAR in April 1968. YA-DAN is seen here on the airline's first visit to Gatwick. (Author's collection)

The only aircraft in the Malta Metropolitan Airlines (UK) Ltd fleet was this seventy-two-seater Douglas C-54D (DC-4) VP-MAA. Originally delivered to the United States Air Force in 1945, it made its way to Germany as D-AMAX in 1962 before Malta Metropolitan bought it in May 1963. Delivered from Brussels to Gatwick on 21 June, it initially went to Biggin Hill for servicing by Air Couriers before returning on the 28th for some circuit training, prior to departing that evening on its first service, Gatwick to Copenhagen. There followed about nine visits that summer on passenger charters, some of them on behalf of Starways and Derby Airways. Founded by Captain Ian Maclean with four others, the airline initially wanted to operate a DC-6 or Britannia on a Malta–London scheduled service, with additional services to Sicily using two DH Herons, but objections by British Eagle, BEA and Skyways prevented any real progress, and after operating a few charters and spending long periods parked up at Gatwick, the airline operation folded in February 1964. The old Skymaster went on to serve in the UK, Rhodesia, the Congo and Gabon before being damaged beyond repair in a landing accident at Kinshasa in 1987. (Peter Marson)

SAGA Norsk Flytjeneste AS from Torp in Norway bought two Douglas DC-6Bs from Braathens SAFE in May 1971, and both of them, LN-MTU and LN-MTV, first visited Gatwick on ad-hoc charters in July that year, LN-MTV from Bergen on 1 July and LN-MTU operating a Braathens flight from Oslo, Fornebu, on 10 July. Initial destinations served included Paris Le Bourget, Basle, Copenhagen and Berlin Schönefeld. However, the airline was short-lived and, having been renamed Troll Air in January 1972, went bust in June that year. In 2018, LN-MTV was still flying in Alaska as N151 with Everts Air. (Bob Wall)

Caledonian Airways (Prestwick) Ltd was formed in 1961 and its first 104-seat Douglas DC-7C (G-ARUD) arrived at its Gatwick base on lease from the Societé Anonyme Belge d'Exploitation de la Navigation Aérienne (SABENA) in November 1961. The Caledonian management had tried forty-eight airlines looking for suitable aircraft to lease and were delighted with the SABENA deal as it included all the major maintenance work. Its first service to Barbados on behalf of London Transport was flown at the end of the month, returning with ninety-five Barbadians who were to start work on the London buses. Five DC-7Cs were leased from SABENA, but the illustrated G-AOIE was purchased from BOAC. It was the last Caledonian DC-7C and its forward fuselage still exists at the Cavan and Leitrim Railway in Ireland. (Author's collection)

Delivered brand new to SABENA in May 1953, this seventy-three-seater 'Super DC-6B' OO-CTK spent some time leased to Air Congo, Aviaco and Caledonian Airways before being sold in Panama in 1969. One of a massive fleet of seventeen DC-6Bs that were often flown to the Belgian Congo or leased out to other operators, OO-CTK is seen here in 1969 complete with a set of BEA steps, nearing the end of sixteen years of SABENA ownership. (Jacques Guillem collection)

An amalgamation of several small Canadian airlines, Pacific Western Airlines (PWA) was founded in May 1953, flying an eclectic mix of aircraft including Beavers, a Beech 18, two Grumman Mallards, three Junkers W-34s, a couple of Fairchild 71s and the inevitable Norseman. By 1956, PWA had grown further, with eighty-five aircraft serving 112 airfields in the Canadian northwest. Its DC-3s and C-46s were joined by DC-6s; some of these soldiered on into the mid-1960s, making innovative long-distance IT group charters to Gatwick from Vancouver and elsewhere. However, this transatlantic service was more suited to the DC-7C seen here in August 1966. PWA had operated a couple of DC-7s from 1964, but the purchase of two long-range 102-seat DC-7Cs (CF-NAI and CF-PWM) in 1965 allowed true transatlantic range. (Mike Axe collection)

Danish charter airline Nordair A/S was founded in September 1960 with a fleet of three seventy-three-seat DC-6s bought from American Airlines, and started flying holidaymakers from Copenhagen to Salzburg the following February. First appearing at Gatwick in June 1961, Nordair's fully owned fleet of six eighty-seat DC-6s were regular arrivals until the airline closed in late 1964. Nordair also leased three additional DC-6s for a short period in 1964, two of them appearing at Gatwick. Scandinavian Airlines (SAS) acquired a 45 per cent stake in the company in July 1963, but despite working together, it was decided to shut down the airline in October 1964 and all assets were absorbed by SAS, with Scanair taking all the tour contracts. (Jacques Guillem collection)

This seventy-seat Douglas DC-4 Skymaster LX-IAL belonged to Interocean Airways, one of several airlines that were registered in the Grand Duchy of Luxembourg, whose central position in Europe and favourable tax laws were advantageous in the cut-throat business of air charter. Interocean Airways was an associate airline of US-based Intercontinental US Inc., set up at Findel Airport in Luxembourg in 1960 to operate a fleet of DC-4s on passenger and freight charters throughout Europe and Africa. Interocean had thirteen DC-4s on its books between 1960 and 1966, but only LX-IAL, HEP, IOA and IOD appeared at Gatwick. The airline also appeared with a pair of ATL.98 Carvairs, a DC-6, a DC-7 and an L-749 Constellation. (Geoff Dobson)

Freddie Laker was not the first low-cost transatlantic carrier with his Skytrain in 1977. Icelandic airline Loftleidir beat him to it by many years, with Douglas DC-4s linking Europe with the USA as early as 1952. Many of these transatlantic flights originated in Luxembourg or Hamburg, where passengers joined for the leisurely but cheap flight to the USA via other stops in Europe, including Amsterdam, London and Glasgow, before flying on to Reykjavik. DC-6Bs (TF-LLE *Snorri Thorfinnson* seen here on 5 August 1966) joined the fleet from 1960, but they were usually seen at Heathrow. Gatwick was a rare stopover, probably after a diversion, with only a handful of visits recorded in the logbooks. (Jacques Guillem collection)

Based at Oakland in California, Temple Airlines made a few visits to Gatwick on transatlantic charters during the summer of 1968, using a pair of former Northwest Airlines Douglas DC-7Cs leased from Modern Air Transport. N287 is seen here at Gatwick on a rainy day in July 1968, having made its first visit to the airport on 22 June. This appearance may well have been on a five-week student tour of Europe, routing Long Beach–JFK–Gatwick–Rome–Munich–Brussels–Gatwick–Shannon–Chicago–Long Beach. It stopped at Brussels instead of Paris because Temple Airlines owed the Paris Airport authorities money for fuel! The airline folded by early September 1968, stranding other US student groups overseas. (Dave Freeman)

Not a common sight at Gatwick, Braathens' Douglas DC-4 Skymaster LN-SUP *Norse Commander* was occasionally used instead of the regular Douglas DC-6s throughout the early/mid-1960s. First appearing at Gatwick in 1960, LN-SUP and its fellow Skymasters had flown worldwide charters since Braathens bought its first one in 1947. This aircraft was sold in Germany in 1966. The airline was a regular with jets into the twenty-first century, but with the advent of low-cost airlines it struggled to compete and eventually merged with SAS Norway in May 2004. (Jacques Guillem collection)

One of two Douglas DC-6Bs leased from SABENA in April 1964 by Caledonian Airways (Prestwick) Ltd, G-ASRZ *County of Angus* was returned to the Belgian airline that November after a successful summer season flying holiday charters to Europe. Caledonian had been formed in 1961 with offices at Imperial Buildings in Horley, Surrey. Its Scottish connection was through its patriotic founder, Captain Adam Thomson, who had been born and brought up in Glasgow. Its first aircraft was a 104-seater DC-7C leased from SABENA, which it flew as G-ARUD. This was soon off on charter work, but sadly crashed in Cameroon in March 1962 with the loss of 111 lives. G-ASRZ ended up in Gabon in 1971, where it was scrapped. (Author's collection)

After Irish freight airline Aer Turas won a six-month contract to operate cargo flights for Italian national airline Alitalia in 1967, it leased its DC-4 Skymaster EI-APK *Monarch of Munster* to the Italians and painted it in full Alitalia colours. After Alitalia's all-freight Douglas DC-9-33Fs arrived, it returned to use by Aer Turas, but retained the rather faded Alitalia titles, which can be seen here in this June 1968 shot at London Gatwick while on a racehorse charter from Dublin. Interestingly, Alitalia had previously leased the very same aircraft when it was EI-ANL with Shannon Air in 1965. The author recalls seeing the last days of this old lady on the fire dump at Hal Far in Malta in 1983. (Jacques Guillem collection)

Possibly the best-known 'propliner' associated with Gatwick through the 1970s and even into the 1980s was this Balair Douglas DC-6A HB-IBS. Once a regular visitor with British United as G-APNO, it was bought by Balair in 1969 and appears to have made its first visit to Gatwick in June 1970. Despite the availability of modern jetliners, Balair cherished its 1958 DC-6 and kept it running regular services to Gatwick up until its last visit, which was witnessed by the author on 25 October 1981. On 21 May 1977, the editor of *Propliner* magazine, Steve Piercey, organised an enthusiasts' flight in the aircraft from Gatwick. With a full load of spotters and enthusiasts, flight BB6626 headed south and routed down to Lydd before returning to Gatwick after forty-five glorious minutes in the air. (Steve Piercey)

A far more common sight at Gatwick than its C-46s were the Transair Sweden DC-6s and DC-7s. Transair's first DC-6 appeared in June 1960 and they continued to make regular appearances until 1965 and odd visits thereafter. After the airline bought nine ex-Eastern Air Lines DC-7Bs (SE-ERD seen here in July 1969) to gradually replace the DC-6s from 1965, they began to appear at Gatwick and continued, sometimes with four movements a day, until 1968 when they were replaced by Boeing 727-100s. Two additional DC-7Bs acquired from South African Airways had brought the DC-7B fleet to eleven, with all of them making Gatwick visits on IT flights. On 1 October 1969, the airline was merged with Scanair and the Gatwick visits stopped. (Author's collection)

Always immaculately turned out, Stuttgart-based Germanair's Douglas DC-6s were a rare spot at Gatwick with only a handful of visits identified. Germanair acquired a single DC-6 D-ABAH in August 1968, followed by a pair of DC-6As D-ABAY and D-ABAZ the following month. The DC-6As were given this splendid paint job by Austrian Airlines in Vienna, and thanks to their freight doors they were immediately busy with long-haul cargo services, including KLM and Lufthansa charters. This pair could also be switched to either seventy-eight- or ninety-seven-passenger layout. Even after Germanair acquired a DC-9 for the summer 1969 season, the two DC-6As soldiered on until they were snapped up by German freight airline Transportflug later that year. (Richard Hunt collection)

Douglas DC-6B F-BGOB was acquired new in 1953 by Paris Orly-based Transports Aériens Intercontinentaux (TAI) for use on its frontline colonial long-haul routes. TAI went through several name changes, UAT and UTA perhaps being better-known names, under which this carrier operated scheduled international services. By 1964 F-BGOB had been relegated to the non-scheduled subsidiary of UTA, Compagnie Aéromaritime d'Affrètement, to handle charters and inclusive tours. During the late 1960s it was one of a handful of Aéromaritime DC-6s to visit Gatwick on seasonal short-haul charters, sometimes making multiple daily visits, bringing in tourists, shoppers and exchange students. Having operated under the same registration and within the same airline group (barring leases) for all its service life, *Oscar Bravo* was retired in 1970. (Jacques Guillem collection)

Gatwick has a long, rich history of hosting Canadian charter operators. Winnipeg-based TransAir only had the one DC-7C (CF-TAY) for transatlantic charter services, in competition with Pacific Western, and this appeared at Gatwick regularly during the late 1960s. Wearing the red and black colour scheme from its previous operator, Northwest Orient, it is seen here parked up for maintenance outside the Air Couriers hangar on 29 May 1966. TransAir took over Midwest Airlines in 1969 and went on to operate some rare aircraft, including the Argosy and the YS-11A. The airline was eventually absorbed into rival Pacific Western in December 1979. The DC-7 is now very rare, with just three airworthy as water bombers in Oregon in 2018. This one was scrapped at Santo Domingo as HI-524CT. (Tony Clarke)

British United Airways' simple blue cheatline outlined in gold was vastly different to the later sandstone and blue scheme that appeared in 1966. This Douglas DC-6B freighter G-ARXZ was leased from Canadian Pacific Airlines in March 1962 for two and a half years and was used almost exclusively on the 'Africargo' service between Heathrow and Johannesburg. It was maintained by Aviation Traders Engineering Ltd (ATEL) at Southend and in 1979 it returned to the British register as G-SIXA with Air Atlantique. (Author's collection)

A sight much missed by fans of old piston-powered propliners at Gatwick is the smoky start-up. Not so much fun if you are standing behind it, but an iconic memory for many enthusiasts. The author can recall times when much of the ramp disappeared in a dense cloud of smoke as a particularly stubborn radial engine reluctantly burst into life, before the aircraft trundled out to the holding point for a run-up on all four engines to check for magneto drop and to get the oil up to operating temperature. The smoky culprit here is Aer Turas's Douglas DC-4 freighter EI-AOR in January 1970. Note the empty background, which is now filled with buildings, and the lack of push-back tug, showing that the crew was going to self-manoeuvre off the stand towards the taxiway. (Author's collection)

Dan-Air London's only Douglas DC-7 was this DC-7B(F) freighter G-ATAB, which it initially leased from Luton-based Trans World Leasing in March 1966 to replace the two DC-4s it had previously leased from the same company. Fitted with two huge port-side freight doors, it was purchased outright by Dan-Air in December 1966. The DC-7 flew ad-hoc long-haul freight charters from Gatwick to Africa and the Middle and Far East. Due to the copious amounts of oil it leaked, *Alpha Bravo* was known by all the ground engineers as the *Torrey Canyon* after the oil tanker that ran aground and spewed oil over the coast of Cornwall in 1967. Later painted up in the more usual red markings, it was withdrawn from use in 1969 and chopped up at Lasham in 1973. (Tony Eastwood collection)

For half a dozen years in the 1960s, the regular arrival of a Braathens Douglas DC-6 was a wonderful sight for lovers of old propliners. Always kept in nice condition, Braathens' fleet of ninety-six-seat DC-6Bs peaked at seven aircraft in 1967. Braathens SAFE (actually Braathens South American & Far East Airtransport A/S) was, for most of its time, the largest domestic airline in Norway. LN-SUB is seen arriving from the west in June 1970; it operated for Braathens for nearly ten years until it was sold on. This aircraft is a survivor, as it was still flying cargo in Alaska for Everts in 2017. (Peter Guiver)

Saturn Airways initially used a couple of Douglas DC-6Bs for military contract work from late 1960. These made a few visits to Gatwick in 1961–62, but in April 1963 the airline did well to lease/purchase three low-time ex-BOAC Douglas DC-7Cs from a broker in Miami. Four more were added in 1964, and with its non-stop transatlantic ability, Saturn was soon very busy on summer tourist transatlantic charter contracts, holiday flights from Tempelhof Airport, West Berlin, and MATS contract flights to East Anglia and West Germany. N90773, seen here in August 1965, had previously visited Gatwick with Trans International in 1960 and President Airlines in 1961 before its first visit in Saturn colours in June 1963. From 1968, Saturn gradually replaced its trusty DC-7Cs with stretched Douglas DC-8-61s. This successful airline was merged with Trans International in December 1976. (Author's collection)

Société Tunisienne de l'Air (Tunis Air) was formed by the government of Tunisia in late 1948, with Air France holding 35 per cent of the investment. Initially Air France transferred some DC-3s to the new airline and a single DC-4/C-54A was leased from Air France in 1954 for a route to Paris. This aircraft was F-BELH, which in 1961 was bought outright and registered TS-BLH. Another DC-4, this time an ex-US Navy R5D version, was bought in 1960, so the airline only had two DC-4s, both of which were occasional visitors to Gatwick between 1961 and 1965. By the summer of 1966, the airline was operating Caravelles to Gatwick. (Brian Stainer via Tony Eastwood)

Lloyd International was founded with a single C-54A in 1961 to fly ships' crews from the UK to the Far East. Initially based at Cambridge Airport, by 1963 the airline had two C-54s and the base had moved to Gatwick. Lloyd's Douglas C-54B Skymaster G-ARWI was a regular sight at Gatwick over the six years it flew for them. One of two C-54s leased from Alaska Airlines in March 1962, it was bought outright in 1964 and subsequently flew almost entirely from Gatwick, concentrating on long-haul missions to the Far East, together with a handful of IT tourist charters. During 1964, G-ARWI flew holidaymakers from Gatwick to Barcelona, Palma, Perpignan, Rimini and Valencia. However, its main IT charter contracts linked Glasgow (Renfrew) Airport with the Mediterranean. (Pierre-Alain Petit)

With just six recorded visits in 1966, this very smart Douglas C-54A (DC-4) VQ-ZEC of Bechuanaland National Airways (BNA) was a rare bird at Gatwick. By the time BNA was founded at Francistown in October 1965, this aircraft was already a world traveller, having served in the USA, Mexico, Thailand and Rhodesia before it entered service flying charters from southern Africa. BNA had been founded by Squadron Leader Johnny Gibson, an RAF Second World War fighter pilot, with some help from British airline Autair. In late 1966, the country became Botswana and BNA unfortunately went out of business. BNA's routes were taken over by another BNA – Botswana National Airways – and the word Bechuanaland was replaced by Botswana on the C-54. However, it is not believed to have carried the new titles at Gatwick after its last recorded visit on 1 October 1966. (Author's collection)

Spantax was founded on 6 October 1959 as Aero Taxis de Espana SA and commenced light aircraft operations before upgrading to a DC-3. The growing airline bought three DC-4s from Iberia in 1962 and by the time of this picture in the summer of 1965, Spantax had seven DC-3s, four DC-4s, two DC-6s, three DC-7s and a Beech 18. On most Saturdays during the summer of 1965, its Douglas DC-4 (C-54) Skymaster EC-AUY operated two return flights from/to Barcelona on passenger charters. (Geoff Dobson)

Balair had first appeared at Gatwick with Vickers Vikings and DC-4s in 1959. This Douglas DC-4, HB-ILD, was a very regular visitor in Gatwick from 1967. Previously a front-line airliner with both KLM and then Olympic Airways, it was bought by Balair in 1967 and flew charters for them around Europe in company with HB-ILA, ILB, ILC and ILU. After replacement by a Fokker Friendship, it was used as a freighter, although it appears to be parked on a regular passenger stand. Seen here in November 1969, it was sold to Zaire the following year and was eventually scrapped there in 1987. (Peter Keating via Tony Eastwood collection)

Probably on its delivery flight from the USA to its new base in Beirut was this Douglas DC-6B N122A with AWA (American World Airways) titles on 14 August 1973. Originally delivered to Canadian Pacific in 1957, this DC-6B was bought by AWA in June 1973 for freight operations in the Middle East. The man behind AWA was George Hallak, alias George Deeb. He seems to have been a 'person of interest' to the US authorities as the Federal Aviation Administration (FAA) investigated him for some misdemeanours, including airline ticketing irregularities. By the summer of 1975 the aircraft was flying for another Middle East airline that the FAA was watching, New World Air Charter. It crashed in Oman in August 1978, killing all four crew. (Bernard King)

Based at Manston in Kent, Air Ferry's Douglas C-54A Skymaster G-ASOG made many visits to Gatwick in 1965–66, although Air Ferry had owned it since January 1964. Seen here on 19 May 1965, it was later painted with a white tail and a larger 'AF' on the fin. It crashed while on a night approach to Frankfurt from Manchester on 21 January 1967, tragically killing the two crew, who, it is believed, had dialled up the wrong altimeter pressure setting. (Peter Keating via Tony Eastwood collection)

The regular arrivals of Società Aerea Mediterranea (SAM) Douglas DC-6Bs at Gatwick meant that they were probably not fully appreciated until they had gone. SAM's fleet (eight in total) of eighty-two-seater 'Sixes' were always immaculate, and from 1961 to 1968 thousands of happy holidaymakers used them on inclusive tours to destinations including Alghero, Genoa, Rimini, Venice, Rome, Milan, Naples, Palermo and Catania. I-DIMA, seen here about to depart for Venice, was the first SAM DC-6B to arrive at Gatwick, on Saturday, 20 May 1961, and its visits continued until 1968 when the fleet was upgraded to use Caravelles. Note the impressive line-up of classic 'propliners' behind. A BUA Viscount and an Air Links Argonaut share the ramp, while a Dan-Air Ambassador and Bristol Freighter, SAM DC-6 and an unidentified DC-4 grace the oil-stained North Park. (Niall Booth collection)

Seen here disgorging passengers at Gatwick in September 1965, PH-DSL *Baltic Sea* was acquired from KLM in October 1964, becoming the second DC-7C of Martin's Air Charter (MAC). These ninety-nine-seater aircraft were often chartered by other airlines, including Gatwick-based Caledonian, to cover aircraft shortages. From the autumn of 1966, the airline flew as Martinair Holland, which gave the company a more professional image. During the very busy summer of 1965, MAC DC-7Cs flew charters from Gatwick to Johannesburg and Salisbury (Rhodesia) on behalf of various travel clubs. (Adrian Balch collection)

Wardair's first large aircraft was this Douglas DC-6B bought in March 1963 for transatlantic charters. According to the old logbooks, CF-PCI made the first of its many visits to London Gatwick on 6 May 1963, and apart from regular summer appearances, it also made some Atlantic crossings to Gatwick with Christmas shoppers. Thereafter, Wardair bought its own DC-6s, and in 1966, a Boeing 727-100 CF-FUN which became a regular at Gatwick. Wardair continued with various types to Gatwick until it was absorbed into Canadian Airlines International in 1989. From May 1966, CF-PCI was flown by Pacific Western Airlines and continued to grace the ramp at Gatwick with its titles. CF-PCI passed through many owners and ended up in Mexico in 1980. (Lee Holden collection)

We have to thank Robin Ridley for this beautiful shot of a shiny DC-6 about to turn onto its parking stand in May 1969. Kar-Air was formed as Karhumäki Airways in 1950, becoming Kar-Air in 1957. As the airline grew, it bought this DC-6B from SAS for long-haul charters and re-registered it as OH-KDC in 1964. A co-operation agreement was signed with Finnair in 1963 after Kar-Air had struggled with financial problems, allowing Kar-Air to concentrate on IT charters. Two other DC-6Bs were bought in 1964 and 1965. OH-KDC and KDB were retired in 1972, but KDA, which had been converted to a 'Swingtail' freighter, soldiered on until 1982, becoming the last regular piston-engine airliner to fly to London Heathrow. (Robin Ridley)

Charter airline Trans-Union SA was established in 1966 as part of the Société Heli-Union to operate passenger charters between Paris (Le Bourget) Nice and Düsseldorf. Initially operating a single DC-4 and a pair of DC-6Bs (F-BNUZ and F-BOEV – seen here in August 1969), the airline expanded with an additional pair of DC-6Bs and the type first appeared at Gatwick in 1967, but they were not a common sight, most likely to be seen on a student charter or bringing French rugby fans over for a match at Twickenham. Two of the DC-6Bs remained in service until 1971, when all flights were upgraded with a pair of Caravelles. (Author's collection)

World Wide Aviation Ltd (WWA) was a Gatwick-based charter airline that operated three Douglas C-54A (DC-4) Skymasters in 1960–61. G-ARIC was delivered to Gatwick from Heathrow by lessors Field Aircraft Services in the early hours of 22 July 1961 and commenced WWA services with a charter to Palma later that day. The airline struggled to stay busy at what was a difficult time for private airlines in the UK and the company ceased all flying early in 1962. This picture can be dated to 7 October 1961 as another view shows DC-4 OD-ADW behind on its only Gatwick visit. On that day G-ARIC arrived at Gatwick shortly before noon, having flown a late season passenger charter from Palma to Manchester earlier in the day. (Brian Stainer via Tony Eastwood)

Regular visitors on tourist charter flights to Spain from the summer of 1963 were the DC-6s and DC-7s of TASSA-Spain. Along with Spantax, Trabajos Aereos del Sahara SA (TASSA) was established at the beginning of the Spanish IT airline era, before the likes of Trans Europa, Aviaco and TAE joined the bandwagon. With a fleet of two DC-3s based in the Canary Islands from 1960, TASSA slowly grew and set up a base at Palma before plunging into the bigger game by buying two DC-6s, one of them (EC-AUC) being the first built, in 1946. The other was EC-AVA, seen here on 4 July 1964 during one of its two rotations to Gatwick that day. In the background are a Caledonian DC-7, DC-6 N100J, the Central African Airways DC-6 I-DIMT and the newly delivered Air Links Argonaut G-ALHI. (Geoff Dobson)

The DC-6 fleet of Danish airline Sterling were always kept in super condition. Here is DC-6B OY-STS taxiying out to the western runway holding point on 3 September 1969. Sterling Airways A/S was founded by the huge tour company Tjæreborg in early 1962. Using a single DC-6, services commenced with a flight from Copenhagen to Palma on 7 July 1962, with the first Gatwick service that September. Sterling also operated a pair of Fokker F-27 Friendships and a single Lockheed L-188 Electra. The first of its SE210 Caravelles, regulars at Gatwick for many years, arrived for the 1965 season. In total, Sterling operated fourteen DC-6Bs, with several of them leased out to Joint Church Aid and the United Nations for relief work. (David Potter)

It is believed that this smartly attired Douglas DC-4, Skymaster G-ASPM of Manston-based Invicta Airways, made its first visit to Gatwick for some maintenance by Air Couriers on 20 March 1965, the same date that Invicta flew its first revenue service from Basle to Manston. On 24 March its other DC-4 G-ASPN flew in for its turn in the hangar and the same crew flew back to Manston in the afternoon. Note the correctly 'dressed' propellers, so that one blade is vertical; this helps to prevent ground staff from walking into a static blade while working on the aircraft. G-ASPM flew with Invicta from 1965 until it was sold in 1972. Invicta had been formed in late 1964 by Hugh Kennard, former managing director at Air Ferry Ltd, with the two DC-4s and two Vikings. Invicta entered the jet age with a Boeing 720 in 1973, but with financial problems and no buyer to bail the company out, it stopped flying in October 1975. (Author's collection)

The Danish DC-7B charter operator Aero-Nord was founded in January 1965 to fly tourists on IT trips to the Mediterranean. That November, it teamed up with Swedish charter airline Ostermanair so as to amalgamate their resources. The new airline was called Internord, and with an impressive fleet of eight DC-7Bs registered in Sweden (SE-) and Denmark (OY-), services commenced on 1 April 1966. Seen here loading passengers under the watchful eyes of a group of oil-splattered engineers is SE-CNG, which first visited Gatwick in August 1966. Internord bought three Convair 990 jetliners from American Airlines in 1967, but the following year the Danish currency was devalued and financial problems forced the closure of the airline in October 1968. (Jacques Guillem collection)

Yugoslavian airline Inex-Adria Airways operated a total of six Douglas DC-6B airliners from 1961. During this period Adria's titling (seen here as Adria Airways) changed several times (Adria Aviopromet and Inex-Adria Airways were also used) until replaced by DC-9 jets in the early 1970s. Originally delivered to KLM, YU-AFC first visited Gatwick in January 1962 and is seen here in the summer of 1966 about to taxi out for a tourist charter to Zagreb, Ljubljana or Dubrovnik in the Adriatic, holiday destinations often overlooked as an early source of Gatwick's legendary charter business growth. Sister ship YU-AFF can still be seen preserved on public display at Ljubljana's picturesque Joze Pucnik Airport. The Adria DC-6s were very common at Gatwick from 1962 to 1967, when the airline suffered financial difficulties and shut down, only to reappear in 1969 with DC-9 Series 30s with Inex-Adria titles. The current incarnation, Adria, became Slovenia's national carrier following secession from Yugoslavia in 1991, flying scheduled services to Gatwick until 2012. (Steve Piercey Collection)

Built as a long-range, 105-seat passenger transport for KLM in 1957, PH-DSE *Irish Sea* was one of fifteen DC-7Cs that served the Dutch national airline as a front-line aircraft for three years before conversion to an all-freight DC-7C(F) in the summer of 1960. KLM called its DC-7 freighters 'Cargo Queens'. PH-DSE made several visits to Gatwick between 1961 and retirement in 1966. KLM famously used its passenger DC-7Cs on a transpolar route (in Dutch *Poolroute*) from Amsterdam via Anchorage to Tokyo, commencing on 1 November 1958. The total flying time was 29½ hours! (Tim Spearman collection)

4

LOVELY LOCKHEEDS

The only Lockheed-built types to be found at Gatwick these days are the occasional Hercules freighter; the once common TriStar wide-bodied jets have all gone, the entire UK-based L-188 Electra turboprop freighter fleet have flown away, and a visit by a JetStar executive jet is a very rare event. Perhaps the Lockheed types most missed by 'propliner' enthusiasts are the Constellation and Starliner. These most elegant airliners disappeared from UK skies long ago, and only a few are airworthy with preservation groups, while others are displayed in museums around the world. The only Constellation in the UK is L-749 N7777G, which is stored inside the Science Museum hangar at Wroughton in Wiltshire.

Perhaps the most elegant piston airliner ever to grace the ramp at Gatwick was the Lockheed L-1649 Starliner. Luxair flew three examples, LX-LGX, LGY and LGZ, all of which visited Gatwick. They were leased from South African airline Trek in the mid-1960s in a co-operative venture, where they flew a low-cost weekly service between Johannesburg and Luxembourg. The Starliners were used to feed this route with regular flights to Luxembourg. LX-LGZ was the first to arrive at Gatwick in April 1964, just after it had been delivered. The weekly route from Luxembourg to Johannesburg stopped at Palma and Luanda, or Lisbon, Cape Verde and Luanda. From June 1968, Transglobe Britannias and CL-44s were leased for the Johannesburg–Luxembourg route, while the Starliners were relegated to the weekly connecting flight to and from Gatwick. The seating arrangement was ninety in tourist class plus eight in the forward lounge. The last Luxair Starliner was withdrawn from use in January 1969. (Jacques Guillem collection)

Seen here on Sunday, 30 July 1961, during its delivery flight to its new base in Geneva, this Swiss-registered Pacaero (Lockheed 18) Learstar Mk.1 HB-AMM was operated by Minnesota Europe SA, the Swiss agents for the huge 3M (Minnesota Mining and Manufacturing) Company. It departed for Geneva Cointrin Airport on 2 August. Just visible in the background are RAF Comet XK699 and Percival Proctor G-AOEJ. HB-AMM returned to the USA in 1965. The aircraft was originally built as a Lodestar for British West Indian Airways, but its long career came to a dramatic end in September 1972 when it crashed and burned in Jamaica while taking off with a load of cannabis. (Tony Clarke collection)

In the summer of 1961, Royal Air Maroc operated a series of fortnightly IT charters to Gatwick, usually from Tangier but also from Marrakesh and Monastir, using Lockheed L-749A Constellation CN-CCP and, just once, CN-CCR. CN-CCP had just returned from Costa Rica, where it had been given a large forward freight door on the port side so that it could be used for occasional freight flights in addition to its regular passenger services. The airline reappeared at Gatwick in the summer of 1967 with Caravelles on tourist charters to Morocco. It was still flying to Gatwick in 2018, six times a week from Casablanca. Another Royal Air Maroc Constellation, CN-CCN, has remarkably survived and is currently preserved at Casablanca. (Peter Keating via Robin Ridley)

Lockheed L-100-30 Hercules 5X-UCF, operated by Uganda Airlines, made its first visit to Gatwick in October 1975 when it was just three months old. The reason for its visit is unknown, but at the time the dictator Idi Amin was in charge and he often used aircraft from the national airline for his own purposes. Transferred to Uganda Air Cargo, it was later named *The Silver Lady* and remarkably was still in service in 2015. (Author)

This magnificent Lockheed L-104H Super Constellation made many visits to Gatwick during the period 1961 to 1964. Los Angeles-based The Flying Tiger Line, so called because its founder Robert Prescott was a former Second World War pilot with General Chennault's 'Flying Tigers' in the Far East, bought ten Super Connie freighters in September 1955. By 1961, they were fitted out for passenger charters, and they made many transatlantic crossings, mostly via Shannon and Gatwick to Europe. N6918C is seen here on Air Couriers' south side maintenance ramp in the summer of 1964. After the airline went all-jet, it made a few appearances at London Gatwick with a Boeing 707 and some DC-8s. (David Potter)

Commencing in 1964, the Imperial Iranian Air Force made many visits to Gatwick with their Lockheed C-130 Hercules. These visits stopped after the overthrow of the Shah of Iran in the Islamic Revolution of February 1979. The serial 5-111 was used on two different Iranian C-130s, but this visit on 27 August 1969 is believed to be c/n 4153. The country bought more than sixty C-130E and C-130H models in total, and as of 2017, it still had around forty-six in the fleet, but not all are serviceable. Much like the Israeli Stratocruisers, they carried high-value freight and probably the occasional VIP. (Dave Freeman)

A regular visitor to Gatwick from 1963 to 1965, Iberia's Lockheed L-1049G EC-AIO *La Nina* was convertible to either freight or passenger configuration. Photographed by Constellation historian Peter Marson on Sunday, 9 August 1964, EC-AIO had already done a round trip to Gatwick in the early hours, arriving from Barcelona at 0057 and departing to Palma at 0220 with a load of bleary-eyed holidaymakers. Seen here taxying in after landing on runway 27 on its return from Palma, it was turned around and off again to Barcelona at 1542, returning yet again at 2359. This old lady was later involved with the Biafran airlift and ended her days at Abidjan in 1971. (Peter Marson)

Back in 1976, the Republic of Gabon had a single Lockheed L382G-30C Hercules, TR-KKA, which it had bought supposedly to assist in the construction of the Trans-Gabon Railway. It made its only visit to Gatwick on 27 July 1976, when the author managed to photograph it while it collected two armour-plated Rolls-Royce Phantom VI Special Limousines for use by President Omar Bongo. After Gabon's second 'Herc' TR-KKB was delivered in December 1976, it also made a single visit to Gatwick the following February. TR-KKA was sold in the USA in 1990, and by 2007 it had become N2731G with Tepper Aviation, a secretive company that reportedly flies missions for the Central Intelligence Agency. It was still current in 2018. (Author collection)

American Flyers Airline (AFA) Lockheed L188 Electra N125US paid a visit to Gatwick on 25 August 1967. Arriving from Le Bourget in Paris, it flew on the next day to Keflavik in Iceland en route to the USA. Originally delivered to Northwest Orient Airlines in 1959, N125US was bought by AFA in 1966 and was one of several airliners used on North Atlantic charters by the so-called 'Affinity Groups'. These groups were supposed to be set up for a company, association or other legal entity of like-minded people who had a principal objective other than travel. However, in most cases, the groups were a scam designed by the airlines to allow passengers to fly for less than the standard International Air Transport Association (IATA) rates. The whole messy situation came to a head when passengers, many of them at Gatwick, were denied boarding as their membership of the 'Affinity Group' was proved to be a charade. The 'Affinity Group' charters were replaced in the early 1970s by the simpler 'Advanced Booking Charter – ABC' and at the same time Laker introduced the revolutionary 'Skytrain' concept. (Dave Freeman)

The author can well remember his surprise and delight in discovering this rare beauty parked at Gatwick on the morning of 1 October 1965. Gatwick could always be relied on to attract some interesting aircraft back in the 1960s, but this was one of the best! Compañia Aeronautica Uruguaya SA (CAUSA) had started operations from Montevideo in 1938 using Junkers Ju 52s on floats. Later types included Sandringham flying boats, Curtiss C-46s and, from 1963, Lockheed L-749A Constellations. CX-BCS was bought from KLM in November 1963 and is seen here on a special charter carrying gold to London on behalf of the Central Bank of Uruguay. It stayed for two days before routing to Shannon en route home to Montevideo, with the round trip taking over eighty-six hours of flying time. (Author's collection)

Probably the most common military aircraft to appear at Gatwick were the Canadian military Lockheed C-130 Hercules that flew in from the Canadian bases in France and West Germany, where they supported NATO in the protection of Western Europe. This CC-130E, 130127, has been pushed back from the stand and is being pulled forward prior to disconnecting the tug in October 1972; note the Canadian Armed Forces titles that appeared around 1968, replacing the earlier Royal Canadian Air Forces titles. The Canadians received their first Hercules in 1960 and the first to visit Gatwick was in 1961. They have operated over sixty 'Hercs' in various versions. (Jacques Guillem collection)

An atmospheric night shot of two Argentine-registered Lockheed Constellations at Gatwick on 11 September 1966. Aerolineas Carreras had been set up in 1960 with a couple of Curtiss C-46s, flying freight up to Miami. L-749A Constellation LV-IIC joined the fleet in 1964 and made only a single visit to Gatwick, flying in from Gander on the 11th and departing to Santa Maria two days later. In the background is LV-IGS (illustrated elsewhere) of Aerotransportes Entre Rios. Note the precarious ladder that would certainly not pass the dreaded 'health and safety' check today. (Pierre-Alain Petit collection)

Originally delivered to Lufthansa in December 1957 as D-ALAN, this Lockheed L-1649A Starliner arrived from Gander at Gatwick at 1630 on 8 June 1968 and stayed until it returned to Gander on the 23rd. Bought in 1966 by the Houston-based travel club Air Venturers, who called themselves 'The Country Club in the Sky', it passed through many companies before ending up with Maurice Roundy in Maine, USA, in 1986. Obviously a survivor, N179AV was re-registered N974R in 1968 and still exists at the Florida Fantasy of Flight museum in Polk, where it is displayed in period Lufthansa colours. It is one of only four surviving Starliners from a total of forty-four built. (Author's collection)

A dull old day at Gatwick is enhanced by the appearance of this elegant, if slightly scruffy, Lockheed L-749A Constellation G-ALAL. Once part of the magnificent BOAC Constellation fleet based at Heathrow in the 1940s and 1950s, it was bought by ACE (Aviation Charter Enterprises) Freighters from Britannia Airways in 1965 and flown on ad-hoc freight charters worldwide, particularly the Middle and Far East. In May 1966, the British dockworkers' strike was a real bonus for ACE as so many goods stranded in the UK needed to be flown abroad. ACE had an office in Lowfield Heath near Gatwick and operated a fleet of dedicated freighters consisting of two DC-4s and five L-749A Connies. G-ALAL was flown to the USA in 1967 and was eventually scrapped in 1974. (Pierre-Alain Petit collection)

A long way from its home at Elizabeth City in South Carolina is this Lockheed SC-130B Hercules '1339' in its dramatic high-visibility colours at Gatwick on April Fool's Day 1961. The aircraft remained at Gatwick until it departed to the USAF base at Evreux in France on the 6th. This was the first Hercules to be delivered to Coast Guard Air Station San Francisco in December 1959, and later the following year it set a distance record by flying non-stop from Shemya in Alaska to Elizabeth City, a total of 5,532 miles. The US Coast Guard (USCG) has operated a total of fifty-nine different Hercules, but it is thought that this was the only time one visited Gatwick. However, other USCG types to visit include the Provider and Beech SNB-5. (Steve Hill collection)

Lanzair (Channel Islands) Ltd had been set up by Duncan Baker in late 1973 with L-749 Constellation N7777G (now preserved at Wroughton) and in October 1974 it leased L-1049 Super Constellation N11SR from P.M. Leasing and named it *Janet*. When it arrived at Gatwick from Jersey on 16 May 1975, it was the last ever visit by a member of the Lockheed Constellation family. Two days later it took off in the rain with the Baker family aboard to make a surprise appearance at the Biggin Hill International Air Fair. In low cloud and heavy rain, it made six approaches to Biggin before seeing the runway, but an oil pressure drop in No. 3 engine caused it to turn around from 50ft and return to Gatwick on three engines. It later made a three-engine ferry flight to Nîmes for repairs, and eventually ended up in pieces in Kuwait. (Dave Freeman)

Undoubtedly the pride of Trans-European's fleet were its two L-049E Constellations, G-AHEL and G-AMUP. Looking to upgrade its short-haul Bristol Wayfarer passenger charter flight operation into European IT services, TEA bought a Constellation from Cubana in February 1961, but this deal fell through and instead TEA bought G-AHEL from Falcon Airways. Based at Gatwick, this flew TEA's first Connie passenger charter service from Gatwick to Berlin on 17 July 1961. G-AHEL was joined by G-AMUP in December 1961, allowing an expansion of routes for the summer 1962 season, but all was not well financially and the company called in the receivers in July 1962. (Brian Stainer via Peter Marson)

Three Lockheed L-1049 Super Constellations, CF-RNR, WWH and PXX, were operated by Montreal-based World Wide Airways (WWA) for passenger charters. Here is CF-PXX on 25 July 1965 being towed off the stand, having arrived from Prestwick the previous evening. It departed back to Canada via Prestwick that morning, while sistership CF-RNR was getting ready to depart Gander on its way to Gatwick. These flights were part of an enterprising series of summer transatlantic charters between Toronto and Montreal to Gatwick, Prestwick, Amsterdam, Geneva, Vienna and Warsaw. However, WWA was short-lived as by the beginning of August 1965 huge delays had built up, leading to the Canadian authorities stepping in and grounding the airline. (Peter Marson)

As well as running group charters to Gatwick from north-west Canada with DC-6, DC-7C and later Boeing 707s, Pacific Western also dropped by with its smartly attired Lockheed L-100 Hercules freighters CF-PWN, PWO, PWR, PWX and C-FPWK. L-100-20 CF-PWX is seen here on its first visit to Gatwick in July 1970 in the south side maintenance area. Note the open roof hatch behind the cockpit, allowing an engineer to get on to the wings, and also the huge underwing fuel tanks that each held around 1,360 gallons of usable fuel. CF-PWX was delivered new in December 1969 and met its demise in a crash at Kisangani in Zaire in 1976. (Mike Axe collection)

This 1947-vintage Lockheed L-749A Constellation was originally delivered to Dutch national airline KLM for international passenger services. Converted to a freighter in 1960, it was later parked up in Costa Rica awaiting a buyer. KLM sold the Connie to Aerotransportes Entre Rios of Argentina in 1964 for US$185,000. AER had started operations with a freighter Curtiss C-46 in 1963, mostly for bloodstock and livestock work. AER flew LV-IGS to Gatwick via Le Bourget in September 1966 on a racehorse charter in September that year. It departed on the 13th for Santa Maria in the Azores en route to Buenos Aires. A second visit, also with livestock, was made in November. The freighter survived until 1982, when it was scrapped at Montevideo. (Author's collection)

This is a rare picture of Toronto-based Kenting Aviation Ltd's Lockheed Hudson CF-CRJ at Gatwick after finishing an aerial survey contract in December 1962, just before flying to Wymeswold for storage. In 1964 it returned to Canada, where it was eventually preserved on a pedestal at Gander in RAF colours. It is currently on display at the North Atlantic Aviation Museum in Gander, Newfoundland. A subsidiary of the British Hunting Group, Kenting was a large aerial survey company started post war that flew the DH Mosquito, Boeing B-17, Consolidated Canso, Avro Anson and even a Supermarine Walrus. (Author's collection)

This Interior Airways L-100 Hercules freighter first arrived at Gatwick on 21 January 1970. The airline was formed at Fairbanks, Alaska, in 1947 with a fleet of small bush planes. In the late 1960s, Interior abandoned its passenger services to concentrate on freight and bought a Lockheed Hercules to service the construction of the famous Alaska pipeline. In total, it operated six L-100s from 1968, many of them shuttling between Fairbanks and Sagwon on pipeline work. In 1972, the airline became a subsidiary of Alaska International Industries and changed its name to Alaska International Air, which continued to operate the Hercules. The full story of Interior Airways can be found in the book *Triumph over Turbulence*, written by the founder, Jim Magoffin. (John Crawford)

Falconair Charter AB was set up in 1967 as an air charter company with a fleet of three Vickers Viscounts based at Bulltofta Airport in Malmö. As traffic increased, two Lockheed Electras were leased from International Aerodyne in late 1968. SE-FGA and SE-FGB were given this magnificent yellow scheme and both were inscribed with 'Sky Express' titles on the nose. First to appear at Gatwick was SE-FGA on 17 February 1968, when it flew Le Bourget–Gatwick–Malmö. A third Electra joined the fleet in 1969 and they continued summer and winter charters to Gatwick until May 1970, when Falconair switched to Stansted. The airline collapsed with serious financial problems in September 1970. (Dave Freeman)

Compagnie d'Affrètements et de Transports Aériens, or Catair as it was known, bought a couple of Air France Lockheed L-1049G Super Constellations in the summer of 1968, and commenced passenger and cargo charter flights the following May out of its base at Pontoise-Cormeilles Airport in the north-western suburbs of Paris. These well-used but still elegant airliners retained the dark-blue Air France colours and were more often seen in the UK on charters carrying Five Nations French rugby fans or groups of students. By 1971, Catair had five Super Connies and had bought its first Caravelle. Its base was later moved to Le Bourget, and F-BHMI, seen here landing on 18 October 1969, was withdrawn from use and parked at Pontoise as a 'gate guard'. It was scrapped in 1975. (Peter Guiver)

Purchased by Aero-Transport from Trans World Airlines (TWA) in the USA in June 1961, L-049 Constellation OE-IFA was delivered from Kansas City via Washington, Gander and Hurn to Vienna Schwechat on 28 June 1961. The aircraft was initially operated on lease to UK-based Falcon Airways until August 1961 alongside its own Constellations. OE-IFA made its first visit to Gatwick that month from Palma and then reappeared at least eleven times more until 1963. Aero-Transport's chief pilot was Marian Kozubski (owner of Falcon Airways), who had something of a reputation with aviation authorities. Aero-Transport ceased flying after allegations of gun running in Djibouti, and Kozubski was later charged with tax and customs offences. Kozubski went on to form Britair East Africa, and then flew for Aden Airways before flying in the Biafran War. (Tony Eastwood collection)

A very rare type to visit the post-1958 Gatwick was the Lockheed Hudson. Only two are known to have landed, CF-CRJ of Kenting Aviation on 1 December 1962 and the illustrated VH-AGJ all the way from Australia. Initially flown by the Royal Australian Air Force in 1942, VH-AGJ ended its moneymaking days on survey flights based in Sydney, NSW. In April 1973 it set off for the UK, where it was to be preserved at the Strathallan Aircraft Collection in Auchterarder, Scotland. Flown by Adastra chief pilot Lionel van Praag, VH-AGJ passed through Gatwick on 3 May 1973, and departed to Edinburgh before arriving at Strathallan on 10 May, having taken over seventy-three hours' flying time from 'Oz'. When Strathallan closed in 1981, the aircraft was bought by the RAF Museum at Hendon, where it still resides in 2019. (John Crawford)

Elegantly liveried with Scottish thistles and the Saltire flag on its fins, L-749A Constellation G-ASYF was a rarity at Gatwick, with only a handful of visits recorded in the surviving air traffic control logbooks. It was delivered in ACE Freighters livery to Gatwick from Cairo on 4 December 1964, and departed to Woensdrecht for storage on the 7th. ACE Scotland was a subsidiary of ACE Freighters, set up in 1966 with this single eighty-two-seat Constellation (which had previously flown with Trek Airways) to fly IT passenger charters to the Mediterranean from Glasgow. G-ASYF is seen here on 4 August 1966, one month before it flew from Gatwick to Coventry after the company folded. (John Mounce collection)

5

CONVAIR, CURTISS AND CANADAIR

The Consolidated Vultee Aircraft Corporation (Convair) was based in San Diego, California. Founded in 1943, it produced some iconic aircraft, such as the B-36 Peacemaker bomber, the F-102 Delta Dagger and the B-58 Hustler. The propeller-powered Convair types most seen at Gatwick were the Convairliners, the 240, 340, 440, 580 and 640. These were operated by a variety of mostly European airlines, but there were also visits by executive models and some US Navy versions. Later Convair types that became favourites to Gatwick enthusiasts were the speedy and very smoky Convair 990 Coronado jetliners of Spanish charter airline Spantax.

The Curtiss-Wright company from St Louis in Missouri was one of many that tried to market a competitor to the DC-3. Its 1936 design, the CW-20, evolved into the C-46 Commando and production started for the US military in 1941. With its distinctive 'double bubble' fuselage cross-section, it had double the cabin volume of the DC-3 and a 45 per cent increase in gross weight. Over 3,000 of this impressive transport were built and post war many were civilianised. They were never common at Gatwick, as most European operators stuck with the Dakota.

The huge Canadair aeronautical company, based in Montreal, produced significant numbers of military jet aircraft under licence, such as the F-86 Sabre, F-104 Starfighter, F-5 Freedom Fighter and T-33 Shooting Star. The company was formed in 1944 to build Consolidated PBY 'Canso' flying boats under licence, and to design and build the North Star airliner, which was based on the Douglas DC-4/C-54. Initially, the North Stars were disliked by passengers as the inboard Rolls-Royce Merlin engines were so noisy, but alterations to the exhaust systems eventually reduced the din. BOAC flew a fleet of twenty-two as 'Argonauts', but in total only seventy-one were completed. The CL-44 and Yukon were based on the Bristol Britannia and again, despite their success in service, only a small number (twelve Yukons and twenty-seven CL-44s) were built.

Taxying on to the 140 stands at Gatwick on 11 April 1974 is Trans Meridian Air Cargo's impressive Canadair CL-44 G-AWWB. Trans Meridian Flying Services (later Transmeridian Air Cargo/TMAC) took to the skies with a C-54 Skymaster G-ARXJ in November 1962, and this made its first visit to Gatwick in February 1963 en route to Brindisi. By 1968 the airline had expanded with a fleet of DC-7CF freighters and was trading as Europe's only all-freight airline. G-AWWB was TMA's first Canadair CL-44 and it entered service in February 1969, shipping cattle to Asmara in Ethiopia (now Eritrea). Tobacco products were flown to Egypt, while fruit and foodstuffs made the return flight to the UK. TMA flew eight CL-44s in total as well as the unique CL-44-0 *Skymonster* N447T. In 1975, G-AWWB was transferred to TMAC (Hong Kong) as VR-HHC. (Peter Guiver)

In late 1964, some former pilots from the collapsed airline Loadair (Sweden) started a new airline with a couple of ex-Loadair DC-3s. Based at Gothenburg, Tor-Air achieved some success and the next year they bought three well-used Curtiss C-46s that had operated relief flights in Africa for Transair Sweden. The new fleet allowed Tor-Air to expand operations including a weekly freight service from Malmö to Southend, returning via Amsterdam, Dusseldorf or Hamburg. Their two DC-3s visited Gatwick in 1965, with the first C-46s (SE-CFA, and SE-CFD seen here) appearing that July on Mediterranean holiday charters on behalf of Transair Sweden. Overstretched finances in 1966 caused the airline to fold by that September. (John Mounce collection)

A matching pair of Dan-Air Morris Minor pickups with 'TRAFFIC' emblazoned on their bonnets attend to this super-clean Convair C-131F 141018 from the Naval Air Force US Atlantic Fleet on Gatwick's North Park in October 1968. It had landed after an emergency diversion with a reported engine fire; the passengers were later collected in sistership 141013. Note that it carries its last three serial digits as its 'name' – *Zero One Eight* – on the nose. After military retirement, this Convairliner went to Beaufort County mosquito control in South Carolina as N4444F, and after use as a pilot trainer, it was parked up and used as a source of spare parts. (Author's collection)

Illustrated elsewhere is Trans Atlantic Airlines' Douglas DC-4 N90443, which, together with another DC-4, was based at Gatwick with this immaculate Curtiss C-46R Commando N10435. The C-46 was used for charters from Gatwick around Europe from March 1961 onwards, but from the end of the year the airline upped sticks and moved to Luxembourg because of disagreements with the British Ministry of Aviation. N10435 was a world traveller. Starting with the US Air Force, it then served with the Indian government before returning to the USA, where it was upgraded to C-46R status, with more powerful R-2800 engines adding 40mph (64km/h) to the cruising speed and 2,204lb (1,000kg) to the payload. It later flew in Venezuela before ending its days in Bolivia. (Author's collection)

A rare visitor on Sunday, 23 February 1969, was this privately owned Convair 240 HB-IMS. It was operated by Aeroleasing on behalf of Bernie Cornfeld, a businessman and international financier who famously asked his sales team, 'Do you sincerely want to be rich?' HB-IMS was re-registered N93218 in 1972 and sold to Israeli Aircraft Industries in October of the same year. It was destroyed in a hangar fire at Tel Aviv in February 1987. Interestingly, the first 'business' aircraft to visit Gatwick was way back in the first year of the new airport. Lockheed Super Ventura N9060 of Cluett Peabody and Co. Inc. visited on 3 July 1958. (Pete Waterfield)

Check out the impressive line-up of classic 'propliners' in the background of this shot, taken from the central viewing area in December 1969 – two Dan-Air Ambassadors, a Donaldson Britannia, two Caledonian Britannias and, to represent Gatwick's early 'jetliners', a pair of Dan-Air Comets and a Condor Boeing 727. Tradewinds was formed after the demise of Gatwick-based Transglobe in late 1968. Its four Canadair CL-44s were repainted in Tradewinds colours, including CL-44D4-1 G-AWDK, which was bought in February 1969. The company ceased flying its last CL-44 in 1980, by which time Boeing 707 freighters had taken over. (Dave Freeman)

This Royal Canadian Air Force Yukon 15928 made two visits to Gatwick in April 1967. It was operated by 437 Squadron, which had originally been a Second World War transport squadron of the RCAF, based in Wiltshire. Reformed at CFB Trenton in 1961 with Yukons, the squadron switched to the Boeing 707 in 1972. The Canadian Yukons (actually Canadair CL-44-6s) were given the type number CC-106. This example was sold in November 1971 and flew freight in Argentina and Uruguay before being written off in 1979. (John Hughes)

Overseas Aviation Ltd commenced flying in the UK in 1954. As operations expanded, chairman Ronald Myhill bought a fleet of seventy-seater ex-BOAC Canadair Argonauts to use on IT services out of West Germany and for worldwide charters from Southend. The illustrated G-ALHN first appeared at Gatwick in the summer of 1960, when a variety of IT services were flown by Overseas Argonauts from UK airports. The airline became one of UK's major independent airlines and the early summer season of 1961 was particularly busy for the company at Gatwick. However, behind the scenes, the airline was in financial trouble, and when BP shut off fuel supplies to Overseas at Gatwick on 15 August, the airline ceased flying. At the time it was the biggest failure in British airline history, and repercussions from the collapse would rumble on for several years. (Tony Eastwood collection)

This airline was set up in June 1946 as a subsidiary of the famous Fred Olsen shipping line, using Douglas DC-3s. As the airline expanded, larger freight types such as the C-46 and DC-6 appeared, and in 1955 Fred Olsen bought brand new passenger Vickers Viscounts. However, it was refused licences to operate scheduled services with them, so it leased them out to BEA and Austrian Airlines. Bought from Braniff Airways in the USA in 1968 and seen here in May 1970, Convair 340 LN-FOF was Fred Olsen's only Convairliner. Used mostly for passenger charters, LN-FOF was a rare sight in the UK, and in 1970 it was converted into a navaid checker for a long contract with the Norwegian Civil Aviation Authority. (Author's collection)

Europe's largest fleet of Curtiss C-46 Commandos was operated by Transair Sweden from its base at Stockholm-Bromma. Founded in 1950, Transair moved into the big time when it bought a pair of DC-3s in 1953 for the blossoming holiday charter market. With expansion came the need for larger machines, so three Curtiss C-46Ts were bought in the USA. These uprated Commandos could carry up to sixty-two passengers or 8 tons of freight. SE-CFA was the first to arrive and it is seen here in May 1965, a month before it was sold to Tor-Air. Transair operated eleven C-46s in total and, unlike its DC-6s, its C-46s were a rare sight at Gatwick. (Jacques Guillem collection)

Originally built as a piston-powered Convair 340 in 1954, this aircraft was upgraded to a similar-looking Convair 440 the following year. Bought as an executive transport by Engelhard Industries Inc. in December 1959, the change to Allison turboprop engines came in 1963 when it was rolled out as a Convair 580. The boss of Engelhard was ex-Second World War bomber pilot, philanthropist and precious metals magnate, Charles William Engelhard Jr. His aviation fleet also contained a Jet Commander named *Pigeon*, a BAC 1-11 named *Platinum Plover* and an Aero Commander called *Partridge*. Convairliner N270E made several visits to Gatwick in 1964–67 and can be seen here with the name *Platinum Plover II* and the flags of countries it visited on the nose. Sold in 1967, it eventually went to Canada, where it was destroyed in a fatal crash in 2006 during a training flight. (Ian MacFarlane)

Delivered brand new as a Convair 440 Metropolitan to Finnish national airline Finnair in August 1957, OH-LRF first appeared at Gatwick in November and December 1959 on Heathrow diversions. Inscribed *Finnliner* on the nose, OH-LRF reappeared in 1966 on summer charter flights on behalf of Kar-Air, but it was still a rare visitor. Finnair is a very old airline, starting as Aero O/Y in 1923 with a Junkers F.13 seaplane; it started to acquire pressurised Convairliners from 1953 and in total operated eight. OH-LRF saw later service in Norway, the USA, Canada, Peru and finally Bolivia, where it was damaged beyond repair in 1993. (Jacques Guillem collection)

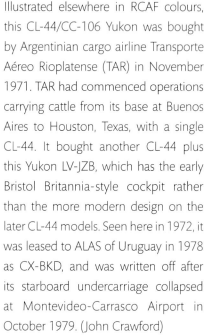

Illustrated elsewhere in RCAF colours, this CL-44/CC-106 Yukon was bought by Argentinian cargo airline Transporte Aéreo Rioplatense (TAR) in November 1971. TAR had commenced operations carrying cattle from its base at Buenos Aires to Houston, Texas, with a single CL-44. It bought another CL-44 plus this Yukon LV-JZB, which has the early Bristol Britannia-style cockpit rather than the more modern design on the later CL-44 models. Seen here in 1972, it was leased to ALAS of Uruguay in 1978 as CX-BKD, and was written off after its starboard undercarriage collapsed at Montevideo-Carrasco Airport in October 1979. (John Crawford)

Making its debut at Gatwick back in June 1959, Fred Olsen Air Transport's Curtiss C-46R LN-FOS was still going strong and with the same airline when it was photographed in August 1970, one year before it was sold in Laos. Fred Olsen Flyselskap A/S, to give the airline its correct title, initially flew with three DC-3s, but from 1957 it operated three uprated C-46Rs on IT charters from Malmö in Sweden. From 1961, the company's main operations reverted to cargo charters, with the airline's DC-3, DC-6A, Viscount and Convair 340 fleet becoming regular Gatwick visitors. (Bob Wall)

From 1952 onwards, non-IATA transatlantic carrier Loftleidir offered the lowest scheduled air fares between Europe and the USA. Initially it flew slow but reliable DC-4s and then DC-6s, but with IATA airlines pressuring it with ever-lower economy-class fares on its 'jetliners', Loftleidir needed to up its game. In February 1964 it ordered two new 160-seat Canadair CL-44s (this one, TF-LLG, plus TF-LLF), which would cut the Atlantic crossing time by 30 per cent. In 1964 Loftleidir's cheapest return fare London–New York–London was £101 15s. Three more joined the fleet, and in 1966 TF-LLF, G and H were converted to the extended-fuselage 189-seat CL-44J version seen here. Loftleidir called them the Rolls-Royce 400. (Dave Freeman)

Overseas Aviation was successfully operating a fleet of seventy-seater Canadair C.4 Argonauts in 1960, and as business grew, it jumped at the chance to purchase the remaining fleet of similar Trans Canada Airlines' Canadair DC-4M North Stars. A contract worth £300,000 was signed for fifteen aircraft on 1 June 1961, and eleven were flown across the Atlantic, commencing with CF-TFO the following day. The illustrated CF-TFN arrived from Gander on 16 June and was pressed into service the next day, still operating under Canadian registry. Despite their similar appearance, the Argonaut and North Star had some differences and the new sixty-passenger North Stars needed extra seating added to match the Argonauts. That July, Overseas commenced a Prestwick–Manchester–Gatwick service three days a week, but financial problems saw the airline collapse that August. (Brian Stainer)

Between 1960 and 1963, Aviación y Comercio, SA's (Aviaco) Convair 440 Metropolitans made many visits to Gatwick, mostly arriving in the middle of the night and departing an hour later. Seen in daylight is EC-APT, which had originally been delivered to SABENA in 1956. With financial help from Iberia, it was bought by Aviaco together with two other SABENA 440s in 1959, becoming Aviaco's first pressurised airliner, and it remained in the fleet until 1973, when it was sold to the Bolivian Air Force. The old logbooks show that the entire fleet of six Convairliners visited Gatwick, even into the 1970s. Note the forward passenger airstairs and the 'Con Radar' (with radar) encryption on the nose. (Peter Keating via Tony Eastwood collection)

Gracing the Gatwick ramp on 6 July 1964, Air Links Argonaut G-ALHT had arrived from Valencia the previous evening and hung around until it departed to Perpignan on 11 July. Bought by Air Links from Danish company Flying Enterprise in January 1964, it arrived at Gatwick from Copenhagen on 27 January as OY-AAH and entered the Air Couriers hangar for preparation work. Rolled out in March carrying its original BOAC registration G-ALHT, it did some crew training flights before its first charter service from Gatwick to Ostend on the 28th. Air Links bought four more Argonauts in 1964 and they were kept busy at Gatwick right through the 1965 season. Air Links became Transglobe Airways in August that year, and with Bristol Britannias arriving, the Argonauts were gradually withdrawn and flown to Redhill for storage and eventual scrapping. (Author's collection)

6

BEST OF THE REST

This final chapter features a variety of types not covered in the previous pages. The Soviet-built types include a visit by an Antonov An-12 freighter. Over 1,200 of this sturdy and efficient cargo hauler were built from 1957 to 1972, but their visits to Gatwick were infrequent. A very rare An-12 in full Ghana Airways livery visited in 1961 and 1962, but no colour shots of it at Gatwick have been discovered. At least fifteen other An-12 operators have appeared from Russia, Belarus, Moldova, Bulgaria, Poland, Ukraine, Yugoslavia and India. The author can recall an Aeroflot An-12 visiting in 1965 on one of his first visits, sadly armed only with his mum's black and white film camera. Also here are some colourful de Havilland Canada Twin Otters passing through on their delivery flights, along with a pristine DHC Caribou on a long delivery flight to Malaysia. There are also a couple of genuine 'warbirds' in the shape of a Boeing B-17 Flying Fortress and a Douglas B-26 Invader. The French-built Nord 262 commuter liner appears here, too. Gatwick-based Dan-Air London flew a single Nord 262 on its Link City network for eighteen months in the early 1970s and it did visit Gatwick a couple of times, but sadly no pictures have been found. All Nord 262s were grounded in December 2008. Finally, probably the rarest type illustrated is the highly modified Grumman Goose amphibian with four engines; its arrival caused scores of enthusiasts to rush off to Gatwick to 'spot' this curiosity.

This immaculate de Havilland Canada DHC-6 Twin Otter Series 200 F-BRPC was bought by French regional carrier Société Air Paris in July 1971 from the British Antarctic Survey in the Falkland Islands. It made the first ever scheduled service to Gatwick by a Twin Otter on 23 August when it arrived from Le Havre. Along with a Beech 99 acquired in May 1972, it replaced the Air Paris Herons on the Le Havre to Gatwick and the Paris–Rouen–Gatwick services. Air Paris was founded in the late 1950s as Air Orly and in 1976 it was absorbed into the Transport Aérien Transrégional (TAT) empire. (Jacques Guillem collection)

Here is an old Gatwick visitor than can still be found in the USA. US Coast Guard Fairchild HC-123B Provider 4505 made its only visit to Gatwick on 18 August 1968, and ten years later it was placed on permanent display at the giant Pima Air and Space Museum in Tucson, Arizona. Like most USCG aircraft, 4505 displays its then base, in this case Naples in Italy, from where it flew search and rescue missions, in addition to its primary role as a logistical transport in support of the expansion of the LORAN C network and other isolated navigational installations. One other USCG Provider visited Gatwick, 4540, also from Naples, on 7 July 1968. (Author's collection)

With only a single visit to Gatwick on Saturday, 2 May 1970, we are lucky that the arrival of IFG's Nord 262A D-CADY was thankfully recorded for posterity by Peter Guiver. With the help of Lufthansa, the government of Nordrhein-Westfalen invested 1.8 million Deutschmarks to create the new airline Interregional Fluggesellschaft with Nord 262s and Fokker F.27s. Bought brand new by IFG, D-CADY first flew in July 1967. Scheduled services commenced from Düsseldorf to Saarbrucken, Hanover and Bremen, but the oil price crisis of 1973–74 destroyed its finances and it shut down in January 1974. (Peter Guiver)

The arrival of three Boeing B-17 Flying Fortresses all the way from the USA via Lisbon on 8 October 1961 was certainly a surprise for the local Gatwick spotters. The Second World War bombers came over to star in the Columbia Pictures film *The War Lover*, starring Steve McQueen and Robert Wagner. The story of their Atlantic crossing was later told in the book *Everything but the Flak*. N9563Z (44-83563), N5232V (44-83877) and N5229V (44-83883) were filmed in black and white at Bovingdon and Manston, and after the filming only N9563Z returned to the USA via Gatwick on 14 May 1962. The other two were damaged during filming, and to save the cost of repairs and the fact that import duty would have to be paid if they stayed in the UK, they were sadly scrapped. N9563Z later became a water bomber and is now preserved in California. (Mike Axe collection)

Despite being a design that evolved from behind the Iron Curtain, the Ilyushin IL-18 was always an elegant airliner and a regular at Gatwick from the early 1960s, with multiple visits by Tarom, TABSO and Malev. Over 560 were built in Moscow and some variants are still flying in 2019, mostly for the Russian Air Force and Navy. Some of these are still configured as 100-seater passenger aircraft. In 2019, Air Koryo still has 110-seat IL-18s in service with no plans to retire them! This 100-seater IL-18V was delivered new to Tarom in Bucharest in 1965 and crashed in April 1977, a year after it was seen here. (John Crawford)

The occasional delivery flight through Gatwick brought some real rarities to the airport. Inbound from Keflavik on 2 May 1966 was this brand new de Havilland Canada DHC-4 Caribou FM1103 en route to the 8th Squadron Royal Malaysian Air Force (RMAF) at Labuan. One of three delivered via Gatwick that day, it departed to Pisa on the 6th and arrived at Kuala Lumpur on the 15th. It survived military service and is currently on display at the RMAF Museum. (Author's collection)

One of the prettiest biz-props built was the elegant Grumman G-159 Gulfstream. Powered by the ever-reliable and long-serving Rolls-Royce Dart turboprop, the prototype G-159 first flew on 14 August 1958 at Bethpage, New York. It was offered with an eight/ten/twelve-seat executive interior or up to twenty-four seats in a high-density passenger layout for commuter operations. The advanced features included forward airstairs and an auxiliary power unit (APU) that allowed for totally independent operations at remote airfields. N1625 was a 1959 model owned by Texaco at the time of its visit on 10 March 1970. (Bernard King)

The arrival of a Boeing Stratocruiser was a very rare sight at Gatwick. Back in 1959 there were a few visits by TALOA 'Strats' on transatlantic charters and a couple of diversions from Heathrow (BOAC and Ghana Airways), but into the 1960s, Gatwick had regular visits from the Israeli Defence Force Stratocruisers. The Israelis gave the type the name 'Anak', meaning Giant. Taxying in sometime in 1970 is 4X-FPY, which first visited Gatwick in December 1963. The name in English and Hebrew under the cockpit windows is *Massada*, an ancient fortress where King Herod's palace stood. Eight other Israeli Stratocruisers were also named after Jewish settlements or mountains. 4X-FPY is currently preserved at the Air Force Museum at Beersheba Hatzerim. (Caz Caswell)

One of several new de Havilland Canada DHC-6 Twin Otters to clear customs at Gatwick on their delivery flight was this Series 300 3B-NAB. It was delivered to Mauritius via Gatwick on 23 January 1975. A second Twin Otter joined the fleet in 1979. This stunning red and white scheme was also seen at Gatwick on Boeing 707 G-APFD while wet-leased by Air Mauritius from British Airtours in 1978–79. Enthusiasts and airport staff have always given nicknames to aircraft types and the much-loved Twin Otter is always known as a 'Twotter'. (Bernard King)

The arrival at Gatwick on 23 November 1971 of this executive version of a Second World War bomber was a nice surprise. Built as a Douglas B-26 Invader in 1944, it never flew with the military and went straight to Arizona for disposal. Bought for use as an executive transport, it was later acquired by Occidental Petroleum as N60XY and the company had it expensively converted to an On Mark Marksman with six/eight seats, pressurisation and a raised cabin roof. It made many visits to Europe and the Middle East between 1966 and 1974. Registered to the Occidental Chemical Corp when it visited, it was one of five On Mark B-26 conversions to appear at Gatwick, the others being D-BACA, N300V, N5294V and N7079G. (Bernard King)

Here is a rare shot of the short-lived Rousseau Aviation Nord 262E F-BNGB at Gatwick on its only visit on 10 July 1970. Dinard-based Rousseau bought the aircraft, the third one built, in February 1970 after it had previously flown in Japan and Madagascar. While carrying a football team from Algiers to Menorca on the last day of 1970, it crashed into the Mediterranean, killing all thirty aboard. The aircraft was never recovered. The airline was a regular at Gatwick, with its first visits using a Dragon Rapide recorded as early as 1963. Rousseau was quite successful for a few years, but was eventually bought out by TAT in 1973. (Author's collection)

This delivery flight to Royal Nepal Airlines from Canada was not the first time an aircraft registered in this remote country had visited Gatwick. Back in 1963–64, four Nepalese Douglas DC-3 Dakotas were delivered through Gatwick, three of them from Dublin where they had been flown by Aer Lingus. A previous Twin Otter delivery via Gatwick to Nepal was in 1968 to the Nepal Royal Flight. This brand-new Series 300 DHC-6 Twin Otter 9N-ABA passed through in May 1971 en route to Paris. It survived the tough operational regime in Nepal for over twenty years before it was damaged beyond repair in June 1991, landing on the uphill runway at Lukla, which is often cited as the most dangerous airport in the world. (Dave Freeman)

A very rare type at Gatwick was the Soviet-built Antonov 24 and its sistership Antonov 26. When An-24B YR-AMR appeared on 19 March 1972, it was actually operated by the Romanian government, but flown in Tarom colours. Over 1,300 An-24s were built and the type was purchased by several non-Iron Curtain operators, especially at the end of its career when the front-line operators disposed of their fleets. Parked neatly on the South Park is 1968-vintage YR-AMR, which remained registered in Romania until it crashed in Italy in December 1995 after suffering from icing. (John Crawford)

A unique aircraft! McKinnon Enterprises of Sandy, Oregon, produced many modified versions of the popular Grumman Goose amphibian, but this was the most extreme. The two Pratt & Whitney radial engines were replaced with four 340hp Lycomings with three-blade props. Originally a military JRF-5 aircraft in the USA, this G-21C was registered in Pakistan as AP-AUY in August 1967 and visited Gatwick inbound from Edinburgh on 23 August while on its delivery flight to the East Pakistan government. It left for Rome five days later. It was later registered S2-AAD in Bangladesh, where it was last noted in poor condition in 2011. (Tony Clarke collection)

Boeing Stratocruisers and Nord N2501 Noratlases operated by the Israeli Defence Force–Air Force (IDF/AF) were seen at Gatwick in the 1960s. No fewer than twelve different Noratlases were noted between 1961 and 1967. Some of them appeared in full camouflage, while this German-built N2501D 4X-FAN was finished in natural metal with a white fuselage top, seen here on 7 September 1962 on a freight flight sharing the South Park with a Dan-Air Avro York. Israel received its first three Noratlas from France in 1955–56 and by June 1967 it had twenty-three, sixteen of them from West German military stocks. The type was eventually retired in 1978. (Steve Hill collection)

Belgian Air Force Fairchild C-119 Boxcar c/n 10686 was modified to C-119G status with different propellers by SABENA in 1956 prior to transfer to the Royal Norwegian Air Force (Luftforsvaret) 335 Squadron at Oslo Gardermoen as 12697 BW-A *Anton*, with only ninety hours' flying time logged. One of eight acquired by Norway from Belgium, it was a nice surprise when it arrived on 3 February 1969, complete with a cartoon duck character on the nose. All eight were given names beginning with their code letter, so BW-B was *Bamse*, BW-C was *Cappy*, etc. 12697 returned to the USA for storage in 1969 and was scrapped in 1976. (Pete Waterfield)

The 1966 World Cup may have some great memories for English football fans, but the Gatwick spotters also had something to celebrate when this well-scrubbed Malev Ilyushin IL-14 HA-MAE parked on stand 1 with the Hungarian football team aboard on 22 July 1966. This wasn't the only visit of a Malev IL-14; previously HA-MAI had appeared way back in October 1958. Although it was a rare type to be seen at Gatwick, other IL-14s to grace the apron were LZ-ILC, ILD and ILE from TABSO Bulgaria. Hungary reached the World Cup quarter-finals, but were knocked out on 23 July by the Soviet Union. (Jacques Guillem collection)

Check out the amazing background in this shot of Nord 262 F-BOHH taken on 27 August 1970. Fifteen light aircraft and a JetRanger helicopter show just how busy Gatwick could be with visiting light aircraft in the 1960s and 1970s. Note also the spotters with their bicycles propped against the fence. This French-built airliner was generally used by commuter airlines or by the French military, but F-BOHH was flown from Saint-Yan by the Service de la Formation Aéronautique (SFA), a government agency that trained pilots for airline operations. It is not known why it appeared at Gatwick, but it may well have been a route training flight. The aircraft flew for the agency until it was grounded in 1998. (Jacques Guillem collection)

Bulair was set up in 1967 as the charter subsidiary of the state airline of Bulgaria, TABSO. Its Antonov An-12B freighter LZ-BAA was a rare visitor at Gatwick in July 1969, as the usual Bulair type to visit the UK at this time was the passenger Ilyushin IL-18. Sistership LZ-BAB made a visit the following year. LZ-BAA was damaged beyond repair after overrunning the runway while landing at Kufrah Airport in Libya in December 1975. (Pete Waterfield)

This sleek and rare commuter liner is the Potez 841. Built at Toulouse and developed from the Astazou-powered Potez 840, the eighteen-passenger 841 was equipped with four P&WC PT6A turboprops, and only two aircraft with this powerplant ever flew. D-CAER was operated by Nuremburg-based Aero-Dienst for several years in the mid-1960s and visited Gatwick at least six times between 1965 and 1968. It was registered N62271 in 1972 for an abortive sales tour of North America, but was finally broken up at Toulouse in 1976. Aero-Dienst is still in business, looking after maintenance of executive jets and props. (Jacques Guillem collection)

Seen here in June 1973, this example had only been acquired by TAT that April. The consolidation of French regional and independent operators in preceding years led TAT to enlarge its fleet and operate services in full Air France (as seen here) or Air Inter livery.

In consequence, Air France-liveried F-27s became a regular sight on seasonal operations to Gatwick. In July 1980, F-BUFO was sold to Air UK as G-BHMX and was retired in 1994 before being scrapped at Norwich. (Author's collection)

BIBLIOGRAPHY

Blewett, Roy (various dates) *Survivors*. Gatwick Aviation Society in association with Complete Classics.

Doyle, Paul, and Pugh, David (2006) *Air Bridge 1: The Story of the Civilian Vehicle Air Ferry from 1947 to 1963*. Forward Airfield Research Publishing.

Gatwick Aviation Society (1967 onwards) *Hawkeye, Gatwick Aviation Society Journal*. Gatwick Aviation Society.

Halliday, Ricky-Dene (1992) *World Airline Colours of Yesteryear*. Aviation Data Centre Ltd.

Hengi, B. I. (1999) *Airlines Remembered: Over 200 Airlines of the Past, Described and Illustrated in Colour*. Midland Publishing.

Hillman, Peter, Jessup, Stuart, Morgan, Adrian, Morris, Tony, Ottenhof, Guus, and Roch, Michael (2004) *More than Half a Century of Soviet Transports*. The Aviation Hobby Shop.

King, John, and Tait, Geoff (1980) *Golden Gatwick: 50 Years of Aviation*. Royal Aeronautical Society.

Larkman, Captain Arthur H. (2008) *Dan-Air: An Airline and Its People*. GMS Enterprises.

Littlefield, David (1992) *A History of the Bristol Britannia*. Halsgrove Press.

Lo Bao, Phil (1989) *An Illustrated History of British European Airways*. Browcom Group plc.

Merton Jones, A.C. (2000) *British Independent Airlines 1946–1976*. The Aviation Hobby Shop

Piercey, Stephen, and later Merton Jones, Tony (1979 onwards) *Propliner Aviation Magazine*.

Porter, Malcolm (2004) *CL-44 Swingtail: The CL-44 Story*. Air-Britain Historians.

Powell, Air Commodore 'Taffy' (1982) *Ferryman: From Ferry Command to Silver City*. Airlife Publications.

Roach, J., and Eastwood, A.B. (various dates) *Turboprop Airliner Production List*, Piston Engine Airliner Production List. AJ Aviation.

Simons, Graham M. (1993) *The Spirit of Dan-Air*. GMS Enterprises.

Thaxter, David (2009) *The History of British Caledonian Airways 1928–1988*. David Thaxter.

Vomhof, Klaus (2001) *Leisure Airlines of Europe*. SCOVAL Publishing.

Woodley, Charles (2014) *Gatwick Airport: The First 50 Years*. The History Press.

Wright, Allan J. (1996) *The British World Airlines Story*. Midland Publishing Ltd.

The History Press
The destination for history
www.thehistorypress.co.uk